A Taste of Gloucestershire

Thanks
John and Angela Sansom of Redcliffe Press, loyal publishers and immutable supporters of local authors. Stephen Morris whose skills with his camera add humour and individuality to the pages and who ostensibly remains unperturbed, whatever the photographic challenges. The kind people we met throughout Gloucestershire who gave us time and told their stories. Nicholas, my husband, who read the copy with a helpful and critical eye. John Urquhart, military historian, whose family farming contacts were a helpful initiation to Gloucestershire. Peter and Cathy Ashmead, informants on many of the excellent sources of food. Clara Sansom for expert editing.

A Taste of Gloucestershire

Andrea LEEMAN

Photography Stephen Morris

 redcliffe

First published in 2009 by Redcliffe Press Ltd.
81g Pembroke Road, Bristol BS8 3EA
T: 0117 973 7207
E: info@redcliffepress.co.uk
www.redcliffepress.co.uk

© Andrea Leeman (text)
© Stephen Morris (photographs and map)
ISBN: 978-1-906593-30-8

British Library Cataloguing-in-Publication Data
A catalogue record for this book is available from
the British Library

Dedicated to the memory of my brother, Andrew

Design: Stephen Morris: smc@freeuk.com
Printed in the Czech Republic via Akcent Media

Contents

The recipes

Introduction

Divided in part by the River Severn and its phenomenal tidal activities, Gloucestershire's rich variety is reflected in its food. On one bank of the Severn, the Vale of Berkeley and the Gloucester and Sharpness Canal run parallel to the river, whilst on the other the A48 follows the river's course, passing the old Lydney docks, through the tree-lined Newnham-on-Severn, itself an important port in late-medieval times, and finally converging on Gloucester. The Forest of Dean is adjacent to that road, chiselled out in part by its colourful history as a source of timber for Tudor ships and by its iron ore and coal mining industries. It still boasts Foresters' Rights, the free grazing of sheep, and in the autumn pigs are permitted to forage for acorns: today it's home to a number of wild boar. Never ask about the bear, that's what they say in the Forest. Amongst the many stories, this one has blighted the people of Ruardean for well over a century. It's about two Russian bears that were brought to the Forest by four Frenchmen – ah, but then I've been asked not to talk about it.

Gloucestershire is known as England's heartland, marked not just by the river but also by the chunk of the Cotswold Hills that cross the county, the escarpment yielding up warm yellow limestone that characterises the building fabric for many of its beautiful houses and cottages. A journalist once tritely described it as Sloane Square with grass, referring to the large houses and trim lawns and the feeling of wealth within the boundaries of the county. It does indeed have a trimness about its villages but it also has an incredible topography with high hills and steep valleys, wild countryside and productive farmland. May Hill pops up in the mythology of the county, famous for its ancient perry pear trees and for its mistletoe. It's said that perry pears will only grow if they are in sight of May Hill, not so surprising as the hill stands at a thousand feet and can be seen from afar. Standing on the grass beneath the crown of pines on the summit you get the feeling that the merest flap of the arms would propel you to some distant meadow or adjacent county. Laurie Lee's village of Slad, the setting for *Cider with Rosie*, is one of those villages set on the side of a steep valley, his grave in Holy Trinity Church facing his favourite pub on the other side of the road, The Woolpack, where they sell Uley beer, the best in the business – and they've even named a beer after the great man himself. Jim Dickenson, bee man, storyteller in his own right, knew Laurie Lee as a lad and remembers his return from the Spanish Civil War.

The Heart of England earned its name too from its many wool towns, wool representing a major part of the county's wealth and symbolized by the Lord Chancellor sitting on the Woolsack in the House of Lords. The wool towns retain their beauty, Stow-on-the-Wold, Chipping Norton, Chipping Campden, Painswick, Nailsworth, the many warehouses and mills now converted to twenty-first-century usage. Today the sheep still graze. Gloucestershire boasts other beasts of value, namely the Old Gloucester cattle, a dying breed towards the end of the last century but thanks to the endeavours of the Dowdeswell sisters of Wick Court, to Charles Martell (creator of Stinking Bishop cheese), Jonathan Crump and others, their numbers are increasing. With the county's rich pastureland, cheese making is of great importance and the cheeses have style and individuality to match their terrain. Double Gloucester has national fame but the lesser known Single Gloucester, for which the cheese maker must have Old Gloucester cows amongst the herd, is a treat that should be relished by all.

Sustainability is the word that occurred repeatedly in this Gloucestershire odyssey, almost as though a Chinese whisper has run through the county. Farming and land stewardship is conducted with a firm eye on the future, as exemplified by The Duchy Home Farm. Obviously not all farming is organic but all the farmers I met voiced concern for their livestock, their land and the eco-system on which it depends. Dave Kaspar and Helen Brent-Smith of Days Cottage are the perry pear wizards, guardians of an ancient orchard, the creators of a new orchard and producers of traditionally made perry, cider and apple juice. Amongst the newer businesses, Jekka McVicar has won her colours nationally with the success of her Organic Herb Farm; it all began with a simple request for a piece of tarragon from her garden.

Farmers' Markets are thriving, as are several of the very good farm shops and the dedication of all involved in the food and drink is magnificent. Finally, I repeat the heartfelt apology given in *A Taste of Somerset* and *A Taste of Devon*. It is to those who are not in the book and who deserve equal recognition, but I hope there will be an opportunity to make amends.

Andrea Leeman, October 2009

The Producers

ABERDEEN ANGUS BEEF

JIM and ROSEMARY BLAIR

Whitfield Farm, Falfield, Gloucestershire, GL12 8DR
Tel: 01454 260334/261010 www.whitfieldfarmorganics.co.uk

Jim Blair, with his leather hat, striped apron and gentle Gloucestershire burr, cuts a dash in the Farmers' Markets with his fine beef. Whitfield Farm has been in the family since 1951 and Jim Blair took over in 1963 from his father after attending Cirencester Agricultural College. At the time the farming was mixed but moved to become a dairy herd only. In the mid-seventies, as milk prices became absurdly low, the farm changed direction to cereal and soft fruit and subsequently set up a PYO in 1980, the Blairs' first introduction to retailing. Successful as this was, the Blairs found themselves pushed out by the large-scale producers in Herefordshire, so whilst continuing to grow the soft fruit, they decided to convert to organic but even the organic farming was not on a large enough scale to be justifiable.

Today Whitfield Farm has settled into a sustainable rhythm of life, something Jim and Rosemary Blair care strongly about. Aberdeen Angus cattle graze the land and live entirely from what the farm can produce. They're grass-fed on permanent pasture and any silage used in winter months is produced on the farm. With the exception of straw, nothing is brought in. The straw, used for bedding, is then composted for six months and put back onto the farmland. There is a bull running permanently with the cattle but they rarely need to sell the calves. Jim's pleased with the high clover content on the land, the healthy bee and insect population and the copious small birds.

A local beekeeper keeps a few hives on the farm. Jim describes this as permaculture-style of farming, managing the land and embracing local resources rather than changing the environment; he fears when oil becomes in short supply, normal farming will become uneconomic – mainstream farming is going to have to address sustainable farming. As he points out, 'it will take a long time to return to this. We can't go on relying on heavy machinery.'

The choice of Aberdeen Angus is for practical reasons. They produce fine quality meat and the cattle get to a sufficient size to make it worthwhile. Slaughter and organic butchery is done locally, the meat is hung for three weeks, any longer and flavours become stronger and there is a texture change in the meat. Then it's down to Jim to go out into the markets and sell his produce, one animal at a time, but he feels things are holding up, even in times of a credit crunch. Every scrap of meat is used in this family business. Jim makes the sausages and beef burgers and his daughter Hetty makes the steak pies, all of which sell faster than they can produce them.

Markets:

Thornbury, Stroud, Cheltenham, Cirencester (in cahoots with a lamb producer) and Whiteladies Road, Bristol.

RAGMANS LANE FARM

Lower Lydbrook, Gloucestershire, GL17 9PA
Tel: 01594 860244 Email: info@ragmans.co.uk www.ragmans.co.uk For willow tel: 01594 861782 Email: info@thewillowbank.com

Matt Gunwell bought Ragmans Lane Farm 18 years ago. On the road to Ruardean from Lydbrook, the farm lies down a track on the right, a stone's throw from Lydbrook and the banks of the Wye River. Its acreage is organic, run on the principles of permaculture inspired by its main proponent, Australian ecologist, Dr Bill Mollison. Permaculture translates as an eco-friendly philosophy used in the management of land: it works with natural systems, embracing the local resources around rather than fighting with nature, and it incorporates life-style such as solar systems, fuel forestry, water conservation, animal management and home designs for energy efficiency. It's a concept that's workable from window box, to waste ground, from country estate to conservation area.

Ragmans Lane has five natural springs on its land, useful not only from the farming aspect but also for The Willow Man, Steve Pickup, alias Steve-the-Weave, who grows and runs a willow business as a separate enterprise on the farm. Ragmans Lane use Steve's willow off-cuts to heat the stoves in the bunkhouse used by some residential workers and students. Meanwhile Steve Pickup runs hands-on courses in designing and making living willow sculptures suitable for garden or estate, including domes, arches and mazes.

Ragmans Lane are educators as well as producing food for the market place such as apples for juice and oyster and shiitake mushrooms. Their aim is to give people an opportunity to learn whilst working and there are some residential places as well as jobs for itinerant workers at harvest times. The apple trees are mulched with newspaper topped with woodchip – and with comfrey. This rhizomonous plant with its fleshy leaves and high calcium content also has a country name, Bone Set or Bone Knit, and was sometimes used as a poultice for sprains. It's certainly considered a bit of a wonder plant for fertilizer, nick-named black gold and grown on the farm around the trees so that it can be harvested three or four times a year and used for mulch.

The farm recently gained organic status. The apple juice is pressed on site after the apples have been hand-graded and washed and put through a milling machine to be chopped. The juice sits in the cooler overnight while the sediment settles, it's then drawn off, bottled, pasteurised for twenty minutes at 72°C to stop the fermentation and the bottles hosed to bring down the temperatures. As well as straight apple juice, there are delicious combinations such as apple and pear and apple and raspberry. Apple juice is a very versatile ingredient in cooking, particularly in sauces.

I first saw Ragmans Lane produce in a Christmas market where they were selling fruiting oyster and shiitake mushroom logs. What could have been mistaken for a stack of firewood were in fact logs with a mycelium inoculation, sold prepared for fruiting about eight months later, either naturally or to be shocked into activity by being thrown on the ground or soaked in icy, non-chlorinated water. The Japanese have apparently been following this technique for

centuries, emulating what happened spontaneously when branches naturally inoculated would break from trees, fall to the ground and fruit immediately.

In addition to learning about permaculture, there are several courses available on the farm from pruning to cider making. The farm is also involved with community-supported agriculture. The CSA aims to increase the quality of food and care of land and it's a method for small-scale farmers and gardeners to have a successful, small-scale closed market, usually focussing on a system of weekly delivery.

Ragmans sell in the Slow Food Market in Bristol. Comfrey shoots can be ordered for home propagation.

BIBURY TROUT FARM

Bibury, Cirencester, Gloucestershire, GL7 5NL
Tel: 01285 740215 or 740212 www.biburytroutfarm.co.uk

Ducks scull along the River Coln, smoke curls from the chimneys of the seventeenth-century weavers' cottages in Arlington Row whilst a posse of photographers immortalize their ancient façades. Beside the bridge a series of well-landscaped ponds, lakes and walkways make up the Bibury Trout Farm. If you've never fished, a simple line and fly are available from the shop, also the wherewithal to catch, gut and clean your own, and weather willing, to barbecue them on site. The eight-acre farm was started in 1902, its limestone water fed into the forty earth ponds from the Coln. The majority of fish are rainbow trout although native browns are gaining in popularity, particularly in the niche restaurant trade where they are seen as a very natural English thing. For smoking purposes, the looser-fleshed rainbows are a better bet, more able to convert protein and store fat and so to take on the additional subtle flavours added by the smoking.

Both brown and rainbow trout are bred on the farm. Bigger fish live in the outdoor ponds, graded throughout their lives for size and type and here a fistful of fish food can set the waters into what is described on the farm as a troghte of fins and tails, descriptive Greek for greed. Away from the ponds a spring provides water for the quiet of the breeding tanks; young gills are too sensitive to handle the river water directly and spring water has the added advantage of running at a constant 10°C. Peter Gray runs the breed tanks and it is complex work. Although some fish are kept for future brood stock, the majority undergo a pressure shot with a triploid machine, knocking out the reproductive part of the developing fish and enabling their growth to develop at a more even rate; it also eliminates the risk of cross breeding with wild fish, should any slip away into the rivers. Where the brood stock are concerned, thirty to forty minutes after fertilization the hatchlings are fed testosterone hormones for up to six weeks to change females to males, thereby removing the Y chromosome and resulting in all-female production.

The farm spawns up to six million ova a year, so providing fry for other fish farmers and for their own stocking purposes. A hundred tonnes of fish or more a year are used to stock lakes and reservoirs throughout the country and over the years, anglers have expressed a preference for sterile (triploid) fish as they eliminate spawning problems during the winter months.

Outside, the earth ponds are drained down and limed from time to time to rid them of incipient parasites. Young fish are vulnerable to natural predators such as crayfish and the occasional silver eel – and the small fry slip as easily down the beaks of robins and blackbirds as the ever-watchful heron's. This is a paradise for other wild life too, with everything from water voles to barn owls. At Bibury the fish are in prime condition, living in good water and with plenty of space; fish will fight and lose fins and eyes if their waters are cramped. Phil Sale, the man at the sharp end in the shop and who also deals with the cleaning and filleting of the fish, reckons they are at their best twenty four hours after

catching, once the adrenalin's out of the fish, but as he says, there are plenty who advocate eating it on the day of catch. In the shop it's all hands on deck. Terry the boss makes the fish pâté and there is home-made quiche, fish pie, smoked trout and fish cakes made by local ladies.

Opening times:
March-October 9.00am-6.00pm Monday-Saturday
November-February 10.00am-4.00pm
(Closed Christmas Day)

Farmers' Markets: Chipping Norton, Woodstock, Deddington, Charlbury, Malmesbury.

DAVID and PENNY HILL

Ruddle Court, Newnham-on-Severn, Gloucestershire GL14 1DY
Tel: 01594 516304 Email: davidandpennyhill@btopenworld.com

On a winter Sunday morning in Bristol's Corn Street, location of the Slow Food Market, I came upon Ruddle Court cheese, tasting a fresh, crumbly version that David and Penny Hill liken to feta, hot on the heels of some of their toothsome Camembert. The farm and dairy lie on the road that follows the Severn from Chepstow to Gloucester and passes through the old port town of Newnham-on-Severn with its medieval buildings and tree-lined streets – and where you can now fall into the George Café and eat panini with aforementioned cheeses.

The Hills returned from working in the Solomon Islands. Initially they went into dairy farming, but as for many farmers, milk prices were so dire they felt a change of direction essential, and the logical way to add value to the milk was cheese making. On the day of my visit, and in an effort to locate David Hill in his dairy amongst a cluster of farm buildings, I pursued the resonance of heavy metal; the dairy radiator responsible for a critical ambient working temperature for the cheese had given up the ghost, so whilst David plumbed, we talked. Milk, rennet and cheese wait for no man.

The Hills learned cheese making from Chris Ashby and Val Bines:[1] 'they know everybody in the cheese world', says David. The Ruddle Court dairy herd numbers one hundred and forty Friesians with the bulk of the milk going to Dairy Crest. I wanted to know what makes Camembert that runaway success we all want to scoop on to rough bread and devour. The answer is pencillium candidum; it causes the white mould to grow around the cheeses and transforms chalky curds to the more familiar-tasting creamy cheese. The maturation takes about six weeks before the cheeses are ready for the markets. Ruddle Court's Fresh Cheese is ready to eat within forty-eight hours and is delicious with salad leaves dressed with walnut oil and a dusting of chives. Penny and David Hill describe themselves as micro-producers and handle all aspects of cheese making and packaging between them.

Ruddle Court cheeses are on sale at Gloucester, Cirencester, Cheltenham and Bristol Farmers' Markets. They are also stocked by Hunter and Todd,[2] delicatessen in the next-door town of Newnham-on-Severn.

1 AB Cheesemaking, 7 Daybell Close, Bottesford, Nottingham, NG13 ODP Tel: 01949 842867
2 See entry for Hunter and Todd on page 126

HOBBS HOUSE BAKERY

4 George Street, Nailsworth, Gloucestershire GL6 OAG
Tel: 01453 839396: www.hobbshousebakery.co.uk

The old wool town of Nailsworth with its steep slated roofs, mills and river by the same name, is something of an epicurean paradise. The building that now houses the bakery with its bowed shop window, terrace from which to watch trout holding the current in the shadows below a little bridge, and the upstairs café, dates back four and a half centuries. On a Saturday morning, shoulder of Gloucester Old Spot pork is pulled from an overnight slow-roast in the bread oven and served with sourdough bread and homemade tomato sauce: their Wild White sourdough won Organic Loaf of the Year in 2008, awarded by the Soil Association. Walking into the bake house is the stuff of childhood dreams. There is a mountain of enormous meringues, hunks of fruitcake, jolly iced buns with smiling faces and crusty loaves dusted with flour, sitting on wooden shelves.

Tom Herbert runs this bakery. He is one of four directors and a fifth-generation baker – and incidentally a Rick Stein Superfood hero! The family business is based in Chipping Sodbury, but for the last seven years Nailsworth has been his particular enterprise, following a childhood initiation of doing everything from cleaning out vans to jamming the doughnuts, succeeded by apprenticeship at Bristol City College.

Walking into the shop, apart from wanting to eat just about everything in sight, the visitor is drawn to the big bread oven centrepiece. Tom describes it as the beating heart of the operation. Thick tiles hold the heat from its ash wood fire. Ingredients in the café and bakery are as local as possible,

including flour from Shipton Mill and the ham that's sandwiched into the scrumptious Croque Monsieurs in the café upstairs. The bread for these is from their famous Sherston overnight dough, made to an old family recipe and using small amounts of flavoursome yeast. The family say that their ancestors slept on the dough bin and were woken for work before the cock crowed, by the dough rising and lifting the lid of the bin and spilling the recumbent baker onto the floor.

Near the bread oven stands a giant food mixer, circa 1950s and still in fine working order. Much of the flour used is from spelt, an ancient variety of wheat grown and milled organically in Sharpham Park, Somerset; many people with flour intolerances find it much easier to digest. The basic dough goes into a warm cupboard to prove. Cakes, buns, pies and tarts are all made in this open kitchen where customers can inhale the glorious smell of baking. Innovation is all part of the game. Staff are recruited with the idea of giving them a thorough training – and it shows. They are helpful and enthusiastic. Was there a company maxim? Tom says 'Put Bread on the Table'. He reckons to make a loaf suitable for every occasion and wouldn't dream of going to a friend's house without a newly baked loaf tucked under his arm, 'more friendly than a bunch of imported flowers.'

Open: Monday-Saturday 7.30am-5.00pm
Café: 7.30am-4.30pm
Farmers' Markets: every Saturday at Stroud.

CHARLES MARTELL

Laurel Farm, Dymock, Gloucestershire GL18 2DP
Tel: 01531 890637 Email: charles@charlesmartell.com

It's hard to know where to begin the story of Charles Martell; is he cheese man, arboriculturalist or stockman? In truth he's all of these things and more besides in his role as conservationist and perpetuator of all things traditional to Gloucestershire. Like many events in life, the beginning of his story was part happenstance; the cheese-making aspect, a hugely successful side of his business, was initially the result of a bit of bluff that went better than he could have ever expected. With a deep interest in nature and most particularly in birds, Charles began working life at Slimbridge before buying the Gloucestershire farm, as it happened, at just the moment when a herd of cattle called Old Gloucesters, almost extinct, were up for sale.

Theoretically Old Gloucester cows date back to the Domesday Book. Factually, William Marshall documented them in 1796 and this was around the time when a member of the gentry, Thomas Bakewell, fixed types of cows by inbreeding. Over the years the herds diminished and a few of the very last Gloucesters were kept by the Dowdeswell sisters at Wick Court, an atmospheric mediaeval farm house at Arlingham passage. When Charles Martell bought his farm in 1972, the Dowdeswells were retiring from Wick Court and selling the herd. Charles wrote – too late – but managed to buy three Old Gloucester cows and a bull from another local farmer and began to breed and create a herd. Somehow the local press got hold of the story about the Gloucesters and a rumour fired up that Double Gloucester cheese was once again being traditionally made from their milk. Before Charles could say curds and whey, the BBC, in the throes of making a programme called 'A Taste of Britain' presented by Derek Cooper of Food Programme fame, was on his doorstep wanting to film the making of the Double Gloucester. The theme of the programme was an epitaph to British food as it used to be. Then – in 1972 – it was the time of change, of imported foods and foreign flavours, hamburgers and fast-baked bread – and goodbye to nursery puddings and many local foods. At that juncture Charles Martell was indeed not geared up to cheese-making. However, the dairy programme was cobbled together for the BBC and a cheese was made. But thereafter the notion of this being an epitaph became red rag to a bull. 'Why not make traditional cheese?' thought Charles.

So began the cheese-making side of the business. Double Gloucester, Single Gloucester, Double Berkeley, Hereford Hop cheese, May Hill Green, a soft cheese rolled in chopped nettles – and the much celebrated Stinking Bishop. Legally, to make Single Gloucester, there must be Old Gloucester cows on the farm and the cheese may be made from semi-skimmed milk. The herd at Laurel Farm is about thirty strong, proportional to the land. I'd always been under the illusion that Stinking Bishop was wittily named for its ripe nose; in fact the name comes from an old variety of pear, named after a crabby-natured local villager, Mr Bishop. The finished cheese is rind-washed in an alcoholic beverage – perry – and the smell develops thanks to a bacterium, *Brevibacterium*

linens that's been added to the milk and reacts with the perry; the same bacterium is used in some of the French cheeses including Époisse, a cheese banned from the Metro! The flavour of Stinking Bishop is milder, creamier and much more alluring than is the nose.

Charles Martell, arboriculturalist, is another chapter. The three counties, Herefordshire, Gloucestershire and Worcestershire are the epicentre of England for growing mistletoe and perry pears. This in itself is a curious combination; mistletoe will grow on almost any tree, yet although not entirely unknown, seldom on pears. But both are prolific in this region. The wiseacres say that to thrive, both must be in sight of May Hill in the country of Gloucestershire and indeed saplings bred in the county and taken to orchards elsewhere have not thrived. Charles has written an on-line guide about Gloucestershire apples,* complete with illustrations. In the county there are also about one hundred indigenous varieties of pears of which roughly seventy-five are in a National Collection locally.

As a man of vision, Charles Martell wants to leave a sustainable ongoing legacy, so part of the master plan is to reinstate a still in an ancient barn, once used for that very purpose. In the near future he will begin distilling perry to make Swiss/French style Pear Eau de Vie – except that it will be Gloucestershire's own. Meanwhile, Gloucester Old Spots fatten in the orchard on whey from the cheese-making and scrunch through the windfall fruits. Jubilee Game chickens, a rare local breed, share running space with Khaki Campbell ducks, housed in Mrs Campbell's original duck house, built in the early twentieth century when Mrs Campbell of Uley in Gloucestershire crossed a good laying duck with an Indian Runner. Henry Hunt, based near Newent, started Jubilee game chickens in 1897; their eggs may be relatively small but they're meaty birds, heading for the size of small turkeys. May Hill is within clear view and things are flourishing much as they used to on Laurel Farm.

Charles Martell's cheeses are widely available in local shops and specialist cheese shops.

* For further information on Gloucestershire fruit trees, Google Gloucestershire Orchard Group: Gloucestershire Pear Varieties or NCCPG: National Council for Conservation of Plants and Gardens/Gloucester Apple Collection. Or consult James Russell's *Man-made Eden: Historic Orchards in Somerset and Gloucestershire*, published by Redcliffe Press.

DAYLESFORD ORGANIC FARMSHOP

Daylesford, Near Kingham, Gloucestershire GL56 OYG Tel: 01608 731 700 Mail order: 0800 083 1233
Email: enquiries@daylesfordfarmshop.com www.daylesfordorganic.com

The concept of Daylesford Organic originated thirty or so years ago at an agricultural fair. Carole Bamford fell into conversation with the owner of an organic food stall, a conversation that at the time, with small children to feed, seemed to make a lot of good sense; why risk chemicals in their food? The Bamford's family farm was then in Staffordshire, preceding their Gloucestershire farm and shop by a number of years. But from the outset of that encounter, the Bamfords' farming ventures took a new route. A herd of red deer heralded the way, providing Soil Association organically-certified venison and also representing the Daylesford Organic philosophy – that everything should be sustainable and that nothing should go to waste. Horns are used for handles on walking sticks and table knives, and hides to make such things as dog leads.

Today most of the lamb, the Aberdeen Angus beef and the venison are still produced in Staffordshire but their Gloucestershire farm has now adopted a herd of Old Gloucester cows, an essential requisite for a farmer wanting to produce Single Gloucester cheese. Daylesford Organic is proud of its cheeses. Carole Bamford met Joe Schneider, cheese maker, who produced their original artisan Cheddar for them, a success that helped put the shop on the map when they first opened in 2002. The Cheddar was followed by Penyston, a soft rind-washed cheese, and then by a Single and Double Gloucester. The latest venture is Adlestrop, rind-washed in Daylesford's French House Rosé wine, Château Léoube, Côte de Provence and named after the local village of Adlestrop, made famous in Edward Thomas's poem.

Daylesford Organic's main cattle herd in Gloucestershire are Friesians, responsible for providing milk, butter, cream, yoghurt and drinking yoghurt for their on-site creamery – the drinking yoghurt is mixed with fresh fruit purées. In addition, the farm grows vegetables and salad for the shop and also seasonal soft fruits, some of which are sold straight from the bush and some are made into homemade jams. On the poultry front, free-range Sasso hens, chosen for their flavour and destined for the table come from Staffordshire; however, the layers are kept at Daylesford and include a breed developed especially for the farm, the Daylesford Legbars whose eggs have exotic blue shells and a rich golden yolk.

Daylesford Organic isn't a dash-in-and-out place; begin in the café, enjoy the smells from the bakery, give in to the temptations of home-made treacle tart and then shop slowly. There is much to look at. The main shop and its satellites such as the creamery, butchery, and garden shop are surrounded by gardens and beyond that, farmland. Their flock of Cotswold sheep, should they so wish, could peer through the windows and see the wool from their coats transformed into rugs, blankets and cushions. There is beautiful cutlery, linen and porcelain to choose from, and handsome cooking pots geared to a long life. I quote from their brochure: 'We are passionate supporters of the Slow Food Movement, bringing back a food culture which revolves around family eating and paying food

and cookery the respect they deserve,
as central to our lives'.

Daylesford opening hours:
Winter months:
Monday-Saturday 9.00am-5.00pm:
Sunday 10.00am-4.00pm
Summer months:
Monday-Saturday 9.00am-6.00pm:
Sunday 10.00am-4.00pm

DAYS COTTAGE

Dave Kaspar and Helen Brent-Smith

Upton Lane, Brookthorpe, Gloucestershire GL4 0UT Tel: 01452 813602 Email: applejuice@dayscottage.co.uk www.dayscottage.co.uk

The old orchard at Days Cottage will soon celebrate its hundredth birthday. Planted by Great Aunt Lucy Kemp in 1912, it's presently in the custodianship of Helen Brent-Smith and Dave Kaspar who moved here twenty years ago, escaping what they jointly agree was the likelihood of a dual burn-out in London as clinical psychologist and language teacher. Helen's roots were here; the land has been her family farm since the 1790s. Today is bitter mid-winter and while the fog is fingering the trees in the old orchard, we talk at the kitchen table. Helen sprints in and out washing bottles and unfreezing pipes for siphoning perry from its storage in wooden whisky casks into bottles, a job that would normally be done in the packing shed, but water in that sink has frozen to a six-inch block while the ground outside is rock hard. Once in the yard, we step into a shed, climbing through a curtain of duvets and into warmth; here Catherine sits, labelling bottles ready for the next market. 'If it's too cold in here, the labels just don't stick,' said Helen.

The year of their arrival coincided with a bumper crop of fruit. 'We just couldn't give the apples away. People would rather drive down the road to the supermarket to buy apples with labels on them and we wanted to find a way of making use of our resources, so investigated making juice. We had geese, ducks and chickens and grew vegetables but apples, juice, cider and perry are now the cash crop. We began bottling in 1992 with 2,500 bottles and now have a self-imposed ceiling of about 30,000 a year.'

Gloucestershire is the capital for perry pears. Helen and Dave confirm the local myth that no perry pear tree will thrive unless it's within sight of May Hill; as Helen points out, you can see May Hill from much of Gloucestershire! Trees that produce perry pears live a long time, up to three hundred years compared with the four score years – and more expected of the apple. It's one of nature's miracles that these tumbled and ancient trees can regularly produce an abundance of fruit. Mistletoe too loves the Gloucestershire countryside and grows on almost every tree – ironically with the general exception of the perry pear – yet the two live cheek by jowl throughout the county. At Christmas Dave and Helen take a Landrover full of the stuff to Westonbirt Arboretum to sell.

Dave Kaspar explains that the old orchards mimic a traditional landscape feature known as forest pasture. 'Open grassland with big trees is a fantastic habitat for all kinds of wildlife, birds of prey in particular. They love hunting down the avenues of old orchards, and there are buzzards, sparrow hawks, little owls and bats. Decaying heartwood of old trees is itself a city for invertebrates, full of grubs – so the orchard has plenty of woodpeckers. Trees are tubes; the living tissue of the tree is the outer skin and the middle is the deadwood so as it dies and rots it becomes a food source for the invertebrates including the Stag beetle and the endangered Noble Chafer beetle.'

Days Cottage Apple Juice is made with apples from

traditional, mature orchards. The fruit comes only from unsprayed orchards and is all picked and pressed in season – dozens of varieties are used, some unique to the county. These give flavours unobtainable from modern commercial fruit and can be enjoyed as unusual single varieties or as carefully blended juice. No additives or preservatives are used and the juice of over a kilo of fresh fruit fills each 75cl bottle.

Some two hundred varieties of fruit trees grow in their orchards. Names roll off the tongue such as Taynton Codlin, the mincemeat apple that goes white and fluffy when cooked, and will not ferment in the jar. Some say linguistically it's the source of the word mollycoddle – simple to digest, easy food for an invalid. And there's Ashmead's Kernel; Dr Ashmead lived in Gloucestershire in the 1700s. A store room revealed a host of other names – Newton Wonder, Gloucester Underleaf, Arlingham Schoolboys, Brown Bess – their various juices ranging in colour from deep pink to clear honey.

The evolution of perry from the tannic little pears to the bottle seems partly in the hands of its makers and partly in the lap of the gods. Fermentation is from the natural wild yeasts found on the skin and the method of production is much the same as that for cider. Fruit is harvested, milled to a pulp and pressed to extract the juice that is then fermented. Days Cottage perry can be sweet, medium or dry and sometimes with a hint of petillance, depending when it is bottled. The juice may clear in the barrels very quickly or it may take up to a year but at the end of the day it's a delicious and traditional drink, perfection with an array of fine Gloucestershire cheeses. Days Cottage sell from the door by prior arrangement. They are at Stroud Farmers' Market on Saturdays and Bristol Farmers' Market on Wednesdays.

Dave Kaspar is Chairman of The Gloucestershire Orchard Group.

A good read: *Man-Made Eden, Historic Orchards in Somerset and Gloucestershire* by James Russell is published by Redcliffe Press.

RED
LONGDEN
+
BROWN
BESS
NOV '08
RRY
NEY RED
OCT
'08
CIDER
YARLINGTON
MILL
DABINET 21 NO
REDS
NOV '0

DUCHY HOME FARM

Broadfield Farm, Tetbury, Gloucestershire, GL8 8SE
www.duchyoriginals.com

The Duchy Home Farm moved location from Cornwall to Gloucestershire when Highgrove became the home of the Prince of Wales and his family in 1980; it was a move that enabled the Prince to be involved with day-to-day running of the farm and to pursue the principles of sustainable farming in which he fervently believes. In 1985, the nearby Broadfield Farm was purchased and added to the existing three blocks of land around Highgrove; in the same year David Wilson was appointed as Farm Manager. From the time that David took on the job in 1985, The Prince of Wales, for philosophical reasons, decided to make the farm organic. The Duchy owns 1,100 acres around Tetbury and also farms land for five different neighbours, so a total of 1,900 acres are now under its organic umbrella.

David Wilson says that at his interview he was asked if he was prepared to try some biologically sustainable farming – and at that time he wasn't entirely sure what it meant. His training at agricultural college had followed the then-current dogma, based on the green revolution of the seventies with emphasis on increasing production by piling on nitrates – and with great attention to correct levels of fertilizers and sprays. But as he points out, that system relied on fossil fuels, particularly on the manufacture of ammonium nitrate, the biggest consumer of fossil fuels in the agricultural system. 'It's not so much the buzzing around on the tractor or belching cows that cause the damage: the hard facts are that it takes an astonishing five to six tonnes of oil and 36 to 37 tonnes of water to make just one tonne of fertilizer. Large amounts of nitrous oxide are released when that nitrogen is applied to the ground. This is an extremely destructive greenhouse gas, two to three hundred times more powerful and damaging than Co^2.'

The essence of organic farming is that it's a sustainable method of food production that balances the needs of soil, livestock, plants and people. The simple magic of its system as far as the land is concerned lies in the seven-year rotation of crops, using clover as its backbone. Atmospheric nitrogen is fixed by rhizobium bacteria in the root nodules of the clover and that is what converts nitrogen into something useable by other plants. Three years of clover will maintain the land for four years of arable crops and while the clover does its underground work, it's also providing summer grazing, silage and hay for farm animals.

When the clover has completed its task, it's ploughed under and the hungriest crop, the winter wheat, is then planted – wheat after grass was just how our forefathers did it. Once the bales from the wheat are off the field, the soil is then planted with catch crops, a mixture of stock turnips, forage rape and mustard and these will come up in the autumn, holding nitrogen and preventing it being leached out by the rain. Sheep then graze the land to help get some fertility back into the brashy[1] Cotswold soil. In fact Home Farm grows wheat, oats, barley and rye; the rye is milled at nearby Shipton Mill[2] and the barley is malted and used to make Duchy Ale. The

mustard is grown for Wiltshire Tracklements in nearby Sherston and is made into Duchy Wholegrain Mustard.

The farm has a large dairy herd of Ayrshires and an Aberdeen Angus beef suckler herd, as well as 500 breeding ewes and half a dozen rare breed pigs. The Prince of Wales is patron of the Rare Breeds Survival Trust, a group that's done sterling work in arresting the decline of rare breeds. Milk from the Ayrshires is sweet and high in lactose and Duchy Home Farm were one of the first five founder-members of OMSCO, Organic Milk Supplies Cooperative Organization, through which some of their milk is marketed. Much of the milk is sold through Duchy Originals, while some of the vegetables, wheat and oats are used in the production of Duchy Original products.

We walked around the farm on a sunny winter day when the farm's Suffolk Punch horses were awaiting deployment to local woodland to haul out felled and fallen timber. Using horses for this task is more practical, less damaging to the woodland than heavy machinery. Over 20 acres of new woodland have been planted together with many new hedges; 'Hedge laying,' says David Wilson, 'is something The Prince of Wales thoroughly enjoys doing.' The cows were in their winter quarters, next to the milking parlour. I wouldn't say I'd seriously swap places but it was tempting. Their manner was verging on gregarious as they stretched out on clean straw chewing the cud while in a far corner a black bull roared sweet talk. Leaving a herd to over-winter outside would not only destroy future grazing if the ground were wet, but the animals themselves like the comfort of shelter. In the very wet September of 2000, the cattle broke into their winter quarters four times; however by April the smell of spring sets them rattling at the gates to access new grass and sunshine.

Fifty acres of this harmonious Duchy farmland are devoted to production of vegetables, the most staff-intensive part of the farm. This was winter and rows of sturdy red and green cabbages were being cut and beetroots dug, ready to be taken to the vegetable shed. The Duchy runs a local veg-box scheme and also sells direct from the vegetable shed three days a week. We discussed the merits of the cheap and cheerful beetroot. David said he roasted them in tinfoil with a little sea salt and a sprig of rosemary so that's exactly what I did and nothing could be simpler or more delicious.

The Veg Shed is open on Wednesday, Friday and Saturday, 8.00am-5.00pm. For further details email: vegbox@duchyhomefarm.org.uk or telephone 01666 503507.

1 Cotswold brash is relatively poor alkaline soil, free-draining and full of limestone
2 See Shipton Mill entry on page 34

DAVID ANTHONY

Cotswold Edge Farm, South Gloucestershire. Shop: 25 Westerleigh Road, Pucklechurch, BS16 9RB.
Tel: 0117 937 4443 Mob: 07812 192361 Email: david.anthony1@sky.com

Rather than selling direct from his farm David Anthony has a shop tucked away in the back of a bakery run by Sandie Ham and from where he sells a selection of his own produce including meat, poultry and eggs and also an excellent range of game. He does the butchery himself and sources foods as locally as possible. Venison comes from Dyrham Park or the Badminton Estate. Depending on the season, he has wild duck, grouse, woodpigeon, rabbit, as well as the popular perennials such as home-made faggots, sausages, bath chaps and black pudding. Bath chaps, originating from the city, are an old favourite and rumour has it they are making a comeback in times of credit crunch. Made from pigs' cheeks, the meat is cured, cooked and rolled into cone-shapes in breadcrumbs. This is the place to go for your Christmas turkey, reared on David's farm, and the various accompanying pickles, chutneys, local vegetables and cheeses.

Opening hours: Monday-Friday 8.30am-3.30pm
                        Saturday 8.00am-1.00pm

Farmers' Markets: Whiteladies Road, Bristol, Stroud, Bradford-on-Avon and Chipping Sodbury.

JAXONS FARM

Hyde Lane, Whitminster, Gloucestershire GL2 7LS
Tel: 01452 740969 Email: beebyac@jaxonsfarm.co.uk

The murmuring in the hen house is a flashback to childhood, the battered pan of warm-cooked potato peelings ready to mash into the food for brown birds similar to those now at my feet. The current chatter is taking place at Jaxons Farm and there are far too many hens to be fed on a few old murphies, nonetheless the language of a contented hen hasn't changed over the years. This is a commercial operation involving four thousand free-range birds whose lives are focussed between henhouse gossip and rummaging around extensive grassland to which they have constant access – and of course laying many dozens of eggs for their keep.

The farmland lies between the Cotswolds and the river Severn. Ashley and Rozanne Beeby moved from mid-Wales and set up shop here in 1981 with the aim of utilizing ten acres of land to generate income. They buy their hens at sixteen weeks and it takes a further month before the birds begin to lay. Production is monitored for quality and weight of egg, and of course there is the usual stream of inspectors knocking on their door, including the RSPCA. The hens are kept for fourteen months, after which laying quality begins to deteriorate. Once upon a time their destiny was for the cooking pot and that earned the farm a few more pennies, but unfortunately imported chicken has knocked down the prices so the Beebys now have to pay to get rid of the carcasses – something of an irony considering the care that's been taken of them in their lifetime.

Jaxons Farm sells many of its eggs through the Farmers' Markets; they've been staunch supporters of the markets almost since their outset. An angle much appreciated by the customer is the fact the eggs are sold ungraded, in fact about as direct from the henhouse to the market stall as is humanly possible. This marketing strategy is underpinned by selling also to a wholesaler to ensure constant turnover. You can't get fresher; the Beebys even tried selling same-day-laid in the market but the hens wouldn't stick to the timetable.

Farmers' Markets: Stroud, Gloucester and Bristol – weekly, Cheltenham – twice a month.

There is a self-catering holiday cottage attached to Jaxons Farm. Tel: 01452 740969: website: www.jaxonsfarm.co.uk email: thestable@jaxonsfarm.co.uk

SHIPTON MILL

Long Newnton, Tetbury, Gloucestershire GL8 8RP
Tel: 01666 505050 Email: hello@shipton-mill.com www.shipton-mill.com

In 1981 John Lister was a businessman in London, but with a dream. His trek around the South West in search of a mill concluded with the purchase and transformation of the derelict Shipton Mill on a little tributary of the Wiltshire Avon. After the Second World War, many small mills were abandoned when the market demand for quantities of cheap flour increased, particularly after the implementation of the Chorley Wood Bread Process, a method of fast, low-cost baking. But Shipton Mill has old roots; it dates back a thousand years to the Domesday Book. Wandering around outside today, ancient tracks leading to the mill from outlying hamlets are still visible; mills once played an integral part in every community. In the 1850s its resident miller borrowed a few French prisoners of war and had the river diverted direct to the mill, avoiding the necessity for a mill leat – the stream of water that's normally diverted from a river to power the mill wheel. Current plans are to restore the old mill wheel to working order as soon as possible but until then, the mill is electrically powered.

Tom Russell is Shipton Mill's front man, an ex-marine biologist, now dedicatedly involved with the workings of the mill and its produce. 'Flour and milling,' he says, 'are present in many diverse cultures – milling goes back to the earliest settlements. Shipton Mill mills nearly 126 different sorts of flour from high protein wholemeal bread flour to silky-white cake flour, low in protein – with a plethora of choice in between.

The millstones are traditional, made of French Burrstone marble. They are not a whole wheel as is used for milling coarser cattle feed, rather they are made up of wedges and held together by an iron band. Each wedge has a fine groove chipped out by the millwright, allowing the flour to filter from the wheel. The grooves used to be hand-cut using a special implement, a mill bill, hence the origin of the expression 'show us the mettle you're made of.' The millwright would show off the chips of metal that lodged in his forearm from the hard work and precision cutting of the millstone. Milling and baking metaphors pop up constantly in our language, for example the term 'upper crust' originally implied the finer and more delicate bread, destined for the high table.

Local grain is milled at Shipton Mill, including a variety called Maris Widgeon from their near-neighbours, the Duchy Home Farm that belongs to The Prince of Wales. In contrast to the grain mountain of a year or so ago, today some of the grain has to be imported. Canadian grain is amongst the best for bread thanks to its short, intense growing season and high protein. This protein turns to gluten when kneaded into bread dough; the higher the protein, the more the gluten and the

better it is for bread as it helps to maintain the rise set up by the yeast. But many people who count themselves as gluten-intolerant are in fact modern-bread intolerant, either to the grain or the baking methods. Spelt is a wheat grain that was known to the Romans and is genetically unchanged; its proteins don't cause the same allergic reactions and it's available both in flour and bread form today.

The grain comes into the mill dry and is then conditioned for eighteen hours. In other words, water is added so that the grain becomes softer and the bran more flexible, making the bran easier to remove. The blend of grains to be milled is called grist, hence 'all grist to the mill' – the mixing of the right ingredients to make the right product. At one time when all the surfaces in the mill would have a fine coating of flour, anyone with the surname name Miller was automatically dubbed Dusty. It wouldn't be true in Shipton Mill today. Despite the constant turnover of grain and whirring of machinery, the mill with its beautiful oak floors, traditionally caulked with tar and varnished, is pristine and as orderly as are the neat packages of flour stacked ready and waiting for customers.

Tom Russell had a useful tip about flour. Don't keep it too long. White flour has a shelf life of about a year and wholemeal, six to nine months before it tends to go rancid.

Shop on site available Monday-Friday 8.30am-5.00pm and most Saturday mornings.

Full range available on: www.shipton-mill.com
Many good delicatessens, farm shops and some independent food retailers either stock or can order the flour for you.

FROCESTER FAYRE

Will Pinker, Frocester Fayre Farm Shop, Church Farm, Peter Street, Frocester, Stonehouse, Gloucestershire GL10 3TJ
Tel: 01453 822054 Email: info@frocesterfayre.co.uk www.frocesterfayre.co.uk

Not that excuses are needed for a shopping spree to Frocester Fayre, but as a bonus to a farm visit, Frocester tithe barn is little more than a mile away and is one of most impressive and important in England, dating back to the late thirteenth century.

Will Pinker and his family are lucky enough to live just down the road. Will describes himself as having married into the farm; his wife Nikki is the third generation tenant farmer on their 250 acres near Stonehouse. He and Nikki met at Seale Hayne Agricultural College in Devon. Until 2000 the family had a dairy herd, but as happened with so many farmers, milk prices drove them to reappraise and diversify. Now the farm is mixed; they have pigs, beef, arable and poultry. The cows are a Welsh Black suckler herd with an Aberdeen Angus bull. 'We've had Jimmy for about three years,' says Will. 'We grow winter wheat, oil seed rape as a break crop between cereals, and then spring barley. We've got our own mill to mix cereals for cattle food, though most of it is sold for feed. All the silage is made on the farm.'

Frocester Fayre is very much a family enterprise involving Will's wife, her father, brother and uncle. The farm shop expanded last year and as well as selling their own meat and eggs, they have built a modern commercial kitchen and butchery employing two full-time butchers who additionally make the farm's sausages, and two ladies in the kitchen, cooking up a storm of ready meals for freezing such as beef casseroles and cottage pies, a selection of faggots, pork pies and pasties. There are also other producers' local foods for sale such as Godsells Cheese[1] and Selsley Herb and Spice Company[2] mustards, oils and chutneys. Will's son Sam, although still at school, looks as though he will follow in the family footsteps. He is already breeding chickens, using different cockerels, and has just got a new venture underway, incubating quails' eggs. He's also a member of the Aberdeen Angus Society.

The shop will organize hog roasts for private parties.

The shop is open: Monday-Friday 8.00am-5.00pm; Saturday 9.00am-12.30pm. Farmers' Markets include Bristol, Thornbury, Cheltenham and Gloucestershire on a fortnightly basis and Stroud every Saturday.

To view Frocester tithe barn, telephone 01453 823250. Open all year at reasonable daylight hours.

1 See page 40
2 See page 61

COTSWOLD COUNTRY LIQUEURS

High Street, Arlingham, Gloucestershire GL2 7JN
Tel: 01452 740681: Mob: 07779 312513 Email: sales@cotswoldcountryliqueurs.com www.cotswoldcountryliqueurs.com

Esther Chapman's business is entering its third year and as is often the way, its beginnings were fortuitous. Her parents and grandparents had made sloe gin and damson brandy for their own larders; Esther followed suit but introduced attractive bottles and gave them as presents for family and friends, including work colleagues. 'People at work said they were lovely. The company I worked for made a lot of people redundant and at the time I was travelling up and down the country working in sales but thanks to the redundancies, had an ever-increasing workload. I felt there must be something better to do in life than this.'

'When the opportunity of voluntary redundancy arose I thought I must have a go at expanding this idea. The business began in September and I was accepted at several Farmers' Markets but by Christmas everything had sold out and I wished I had more stock. The first four months of the year are very quiet as people are either paying off Christmas debts or on a de-tox and from April to September the business is part-time with a few country and food shows. October to December is constantly busy in all the Farmers' Markets, charity and Christmas fairs.'

Most of Esther's fruit is gathered locally. As she says, it's useful having two large dogs that need walking as the fruit gathering includes wild sloes, blackberries and damsons; many of her raspberries come from two ladies in the village and the Morello cherries from another contact with productive Morello trees. Any seasonal surplus fruit is bagged up and frozen in appropriate quantities to facilitate the making of the liqueurs throughout the year. The base spirits are those one might use at home – gin, vodka, brandy and whisky. She says she's sometimes told her liqueurs are expensive compared with supermarket ones, but as Esther points out, the supermarkets mass-produce using a sugar syrup, with the result that the liqueur is diluted and lower in alcohol, so less intensely flavoured. The higher the alcohol by volume, the longer the fruit holds its flavour.

The liqueurs are elegant in their slim 35cl bottles, ranging from Elderflower and Lemon to Quince – and for Christmas, a Cranberry and Orange special. I commented on the professional labelling. Uncertain of how to go about this, Esther approached the marketing manager of Three Choirs Vineyard who put her in touch with Simon Day of Western Cider and a master at design and web sites. The Cherry Brandy and Sloe Gin have won Taste of the West Awards, but Damson Brandy is the top favourite with customers. Esther's recommendation is to serve the almost port-like Damson with cheese. She suggests the Quince Liqueur over ice as an aperitif and her speciality, Cotswold Kir, the Blackberry Liqueur, with a sparkling wine; a splash of Raspberry gives panache to any summer pudding.

Esther Chapman sells fortnightly at Cirencester and Cheltenham Farmers' Markets and at Stroud Farmers' Market from October. Details of other events are on the 'Where to Buy' page of her website.

GODSELLS CHEESE

Liz Godsell and Bryan McNab-Jones, Dougalls, Church Road, Leonard Stanley, Stonehouse, Gloucestershire GL10 3NP
Tel: 01453 827802 Email: godsellscheese@btinternet.com www.godsellscheese.co.uk

Liz Godsell is a farmer; she is also a cheese lover and a Master Cheesemaker. For the last 200 years, a member of her family has been at Church Farm, situated below a long line of Gloucestershire escarpment. However the expectation was that when Liz married, one or other of her brothers would take over the farm and that she would become, well, maybe a farmer's wife elsewhere. After she had taken a degree in Agriculture at Aberystwyth University where she met her husband Bryan McNab-Jones, her father hesitantly allowed her to come back to work on the farm, thinking she wouldn't last more than a year. Her father had started the dairy farm with Shorthorns and Friesians and recently Liz added the still rare Old Gloucester cattle to the herd when the decision was made to produce Single Gloucester cheese.

Prior to 2001, Church Farm's milk was sold to Dairycrest, but milk prices reached a catastrophic low of 16p a litre and a rapid decision had to be made about the business – whether to stay in and rethink, or to get out. Around this time, *Farmers' Weekly* ran an advertisement for places at Cannington College in Somerset, offering a Dairy Processing Course that would be funded by Europe and would require a commitment of one day a week for a year; the course covered everything that can be done with milk. Liz decided to take the course and to begin making cheeses.

'Cheese was once the poor man's food,' she says. 'Long ago, if a farmer wanted a bit of cash, he'd skim the cream off the afternoon's milk to make the butter and that would leave him with skimmed milk. The following day he'd mix the skimmed milk with the morning's full cream milk and with the blend, he would make Single Gloucester cheese. Single Gloucester cheeses mature faster than Double Gloucesters and we sell ours at about four months old; some people sell them after six to eight weeks old, but the extra age makes ours a little different. Today, in order to make a Single Gloucester, you must have Old Gloucester cows on the farm although their milk can be blended with milk from the rest of the herd. This might sound a bit complicated but the particular EU legislation is called PDO, Protected Designated Origin, and helps both to ensure the survival of these rare cattle and to guarantee the origin of the food.'

The conversation moved to Double Gloucester. 'If the cheese was made with the full complement of milk and cream from both morning and afternoon milking, then the cheese was entitled to be a Double Gloucester, and just to show there'd been no scrimping with the cream, farmers added extract from the seeds of the Annatto bean to give it even greater colour, though some people say it was put in to cover up mistakes! Annatto bean is from a tropical South American tree and gives the orangey colour seen in Double Gloucester. William Marshall, who wrote about the rural economy in Gloucestershire in the 1790s, said that the cost of Annatto was so high that the cheeses were actually judged on their colour rather than flavour. Some say carrot was used as a substitute.

'I am definitely a fresh crusty-bread-and-cheese person,

rather than cheese with fancy biscuits,' says Liz, 'and I like to accompany it with still or sparkling apple juice or white wine – with the exception of our Scary Mary. Scary Mary is the sort of cheese to eat at the end of a meal with a glass of good single malt whisky.' Like many good things in life, Scary Mary evolved by accident. The aim had been to make a Vignotte-style cheese (Church Farm's version is called Nymphsfield) that would be sold at about ten days old, but a few were left over after a market and one evening around the table they were produced from a dark corner in the cheese store, by then little black hairy balls. 'Scary,' said a friend, but the cheeses were deemed delicious. Holy Smoke is another cheese unique to Godsells, a little like a Single Gloucester and smoked on their farm using oak and beech wood.

There was a phone call from the dairy. Wheels of Single Gloucester were ready to be lifted from their moulds and bound in muslin, prior to maturation in the cheese store: heavy work and requiring a full team effort from Liz and her cheese makers.

Godsells cheeses are on sale weekly at Stroud Farmers' Markets. They are also sold in a number of shops including Todd and Hunter in Newnham-on-Severn and The House of Cheese in Tetbury.

HAYLES FRUIT FARM

Martin Harrell, Winchcombe, Gloucestershire, GL54 5PB
Tel: 01242 602123 Email: info@hayles-fruit-farm.co.uk www.hayles-fruit-farm.co.uk

On the boundary with the fertile Vale of Evesham, the countryside encompassing Hayles Fruit Farm near Haile Abbey taps into a clay loam soil, a good growing medium for fruit trees and bushes and reasonable for the soft fruits. This area was once the domain of the Sudeley family, the site originally a family business set up by Lord Sudeley in 1880 when he owned Toddington Manor; Damien Hirst has purchased it recently and it's in the process of refurbishment. Lord Sudeley founded the Toddington Orchard Company and planted up a vast number of farms and orchards but today all except one have been grubbed up; only Hayles Fruit Farm survives to tell the tale of old orchard glories. Lord Sudeley, a natural eccentric, ran into financial problems during the great agricultural depression and despite his land assets, Lloyds Bank filed for bankruptcy in 1893. Ultimately the opportunity to purchase the farm came the way of Martin Harrell's father.

The farm is large, 135 acres of which about 50 acres are apples, pears and plums with fifteen acres of soft and bush fruit. Cob nuts have been a speciality of the farm, planted originally in Lord Sudeley's day, but the trees have been struggling with the advent of milder, wetter winters. Cobs are the same as a filbert nut, a bit bigger than a hazel and delicious when eaten green and crunchy in the early autumn. In fact it's been a tough few years for the farm, having just experienced one of the worst harvests since the war. The combination of cold and then the flooding in 2007 affected the trees just at the moment when they were forming fruit buds for the following season. Martin's prognosis for the cob nuts in 2009 is not a lot better, 'the catkins available this year are not fantastic'.

If the fickle climate changes were not sufficient disruption, raspberries too face a new predicament. In the last year or so many crops have contracted a fungal root rot called phytophthora, a similar but slightly different strain to that affecting the oak trees. The raspberry problem is nationwide but Mike Harrell thinks in the case of the farm, it's being transmitted through their irrigation system and the only solution is to put the raspberries into growing pots and to water direct from the mains. Fortunately blackcurrants and strawberries remain unaffected. Weather is a constant anxiety; one year a rogue hail storm caused pitting in almost an entire apple crop but at least this led inadvertently to a new line of the business, apple juice and cider, made on the premises and proving enduringly popular.

Orchards are beautiful throughout all the seasons and the grand sweep up the hill through the trees to the line of pines that act as a windbreak is magnificent. Difficult seasons have led to new initiatives such as the farm's café-restaurant where

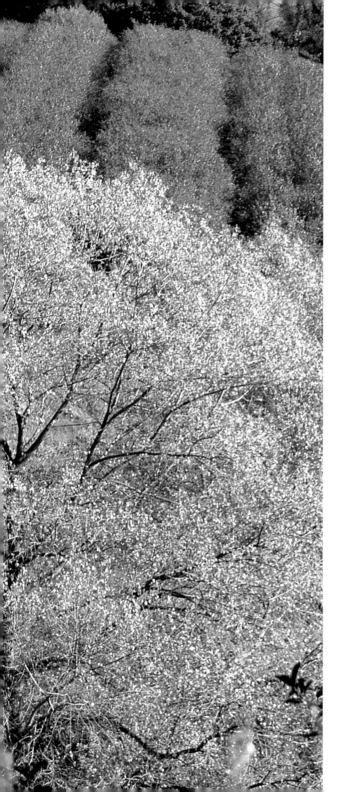

a seat in the window looks out on the bird life and a venerable Bramley apple tree, gnarled as an old soothsayer. The PYO is always a favourite, as is the farm shop with its home-grown seasonal produce such as Victoria and Marjorie's Seedling plums, Conference and Comice pears and Bramley and Blenheim Orange apples, together with the cider, soft fruits, apple juice and many other locally produced foods.

Open: PYO in season, 9.00am-5.00pm
Shop: closed on Mondays, January-March, otherwise open daily 9.00am-5.00pm
Camping: all year round.

JIM DICKENSON and SONS

Stancombe Beech Farm, Stancombe Lane, Stroud, Gloucestershire GL6 7NF
Tel: 01452 770501

Jim Dickenson, raconteur and bee farmer, was born in the village of Slad. He says one of his earliest memories was having Laurie Lee and Laurie Lee's brother pointed out to him by the school teacher, not because Laurie Lee was famous – this was many years before he wrote *Cider with Rosie* – rather that he was a village lad who'd just come back from the Spanish Civil War. Jim reckons he himself was about eight at the time. 'Things were hard then,' he recalls. 'We didn't have a bathroom, just a tin bath under the kitchen table and the Cotswold privy at the end of the garden. Bath day was just once a week, me first, then my mother and my father last because he worked outdoors and was the dirtiest – we all shared the water in those days.' While he was outside playing cricket with two school friends, a swarm of bees flew over and caught Jim's eye; that was between prodding wasps' nests with sticks and discovering that if the boys went back a second time, the wasps would attack. 'Like bees, they're intelligent. When I was in High School, my teacher Miss Otley must have known a beekeeper because she had an observation hive put in the classroom with a hole in the window so the bees could fly in and out. Imagine that happening today with Health and Safety regulations! I used to spend as much time as possible watching the bees rather than doing my school work. I could pick out the Queen and the twelve nurse bees all around her; they'd be feeding her with nectar, grooming her and cleaning out all the cells for her to lay her eggs.'

The next move was to Marling Grammar School and then to Wycliffe College, 'where we were evacuated to Lampeter in Wales. I joined the Young Farmers there. The master in charge was the woodwork master, Whacker Bullock we called him; he used to whack us round the head from time to time. The school had seven hives of bees in WBC hives[1] and as I wasn't very academic, when the bees swarmed they'd let me help catch the swarms. I got sent on a five-mile walk for stealing birds' eggs and putting them up the dormitory chimney too. We must have spent a lot of time out of doors then, I remember going with the Scouts and we walked up the Pig Path to the top of Snowdon, right up into the clouds and all the way down again.'

Today Jim and his wife Vi's son Keith helps them with the bees. Keith and his brother Ashley run the family farm, growing vegetables, including eight acres of potatoes, all hand-gathered to avoid damage or bruising. This was a spring day and Jim had spotted the first few bees flying around. 'Got to watch your washing if you put it next to bee hives. Even in the winter, every three weeks, the bees have to come out and empty themselves so you can end up with nasty little spots on

your clean clothes.' The bees he'd seen earlier were probably after early pollen from catkins or pussy willow, although the first real flow of nectar is from dandelions. 'They'll travel up to three miles for oil seed rape; that makes good honey, but it's better when it matures, it goes softer. We made three tonnes of honey last year.'

Varroa mite is a problem, as it is for all bee farmers and beekeepers. Jim reckons the term beekeeper really applies to enthusiastic amateurs or those with just a few hives; bee farmers are those with over forty hives. A friend of Keith's had taken photographs of the mites, vicious little crab-like creatures that were responsible for the loss of twenty per cent of their bees last year and they reckon it could be up to thirty per cent this year. We set out to look at a few hives. 'You won't mind my shed will you,' said Jim. 'I keep spiders in there. I met a lady from Jersey who told me spiders help to control wax moth – a pest that gets into the fabric of the hives.' Jim's den was no place for arachnophobes; indeed the shed was festooned with cobwebs, but on close inspection of hives awaiting repair, not a wax moth in sight.

2008 was apparently a good year for mating, there were a lot of Queen bees around, but the weather was against them. The crucial period for honey is the last week in June and the first two weeks in July. 'You have to be careful when taking

the honey away from the hives as the bees can starve as easily in summer as they can in winter. I feed them ambrosia, sugar and water.' In total the Dickensons have twenty-eight sites for their hives, including some on Exmoor in order to make the much-coveted heather honey.

'It's been a wonderful life. The birds and the bees go together. We have a bit of trouble with woodpeckers because they can go through a hive just like a drill, with bits of wood flying everywhere. Then they eat the grubs and the bees. Even mice will go and live in the hive in winter but they'll get stung to death in spring. Tom Tits will tap the hive with their beaks and when the bee comes out, they'll eat it and all you find is a pile of wings. A hive in the summer is a bit like a dryer. The honey's got about seventy per cent moisture in it and on a warm night you can hear the humming all night; some of the bees have their bottoms facing one way and some the other as they fan away the moisture. The nurse bees in the hive will run the honey up and down their probosces to take the water out. If they've been taking fragrant nectar, lovely smells come out of the hive sometimes.'

Like Jim, Keith makes his honey at night when it's cooler and there's less interruption from bees, wasps and other insects. Just before I left, father and son opened a jar of ivy honey for me to taste – strong, sweet and eerily redolent of walking on a late autumn day when the flowers smell so strong. Ivy is one of nature's most important plants Jim reckons. The sweet-smelling flowers are the last in the year, thus the final feed the bees get before winter; its foliage is a habitat for insects and birds and the berries, a feast for the latter. Keith says honey is superfood. As one who has eaten a spoonful of honey every morning of my adult life, I can only agree.

Lypiatt Lodge Honey is available from many outlets including the Dickensons' Farm Shop at Stancombe Beech Farm and at Sunshine Health in Stroud.

Opening hours for Farm Shop:
Monday-Wednesday 8.30am-1.00pm
Thursday-Friday 8.30am-1.00pm: 2.00pm-5.30pm
Saturday 8.30am-1.00pm: Sunday 9.00am-12.30pm

1 WBC hives are named after their creator, William Broughton Carr. They are classic double-walled hives and look rather like pyramids, stacked one on top of another. Today they are mostly replaced by a simpler style of hive.

JEKKA McVICAR

Rose Cottage, Shellards Lane, Alveston, South Gloucestershire BS35 3SY
Tel: 01454 418878, 0845 290 3255 Email: sales@jekkasherbfarm.com www.jekkasherbfarm.com

Jekka McVicar was born with green fingers and lots of energy; she is also unstinting in her praise for her hard-working team who sow, pot, water, nurture and pack the multitude of herbs grown on the farm. Jekka is from a potent lineage of gardeners, artists and cooks, and is one of this country's most successful herb growers and authors on the subject. Her great-grandfather spent considerably more than his last farthing collecting rhododendrons, her father was an artist and a collector of tree peonies, her mother and grandmother were cooks and her great aunt, Anne Hewer together with husband Tom Hewer, who was a pathologist, owned Vine House in Henbury, Bristol famous to many gardeners for its exquisite collection of plants and trees. Jekka herself went to art school and her daughter, Hannah McVicar who has inherited the family's artistic flair, has beautifully illustrated her mother's catalogues and books.

For Jekka, the horticulture began at school where she had a garden, but the concept that gardening might become a commercial proposition occurred much later as an adult when she was at home with her young children. A friend came round to beg a piece of tarragon for an Elizabeth David recipe. 'That was 26 years ago and I said help yourself, and thought, phew, you can't buy that anywhere so why don't I grow it and sell it? It all started from there. I began supplying greengrocers in Bristol and a garden centre, but the nursery became too stretched. That's when we began to sell the plants by mail order, which is where we are today.'

We stepped out into the nursery, Jekka followed by Hampton, the dog she describes as her alter ego. The Herb Farm exhibits at two shows a year, Chelsea and Hampton Court. When Jekka began exhibiting at Chelsea, she set herself a target of winning 60 gold medals, and passed the target last year after only 15 years. 2009 has seen the addition of another gold at Chelsea, a grand way to exit the Flower Show as she disclosed it was to be her Last Stand there. The farm is fully organic and apart from using one glasshouse as protection from frost, the plant-rearing areas are 'as cold as nature intended. We are totally dependent on the seasons; there is no trickery involved. They are not like supermarket herbs that are twenty-four days from seed to sale and far more delicate.' I asked about the problems of organics and controlling the slugs and snails. 'We have integrated pest management; basically we'll introduce a predator. Now you can get a predator for anything, it's amazing! We don't use many because it costs a fortune but I'm a huge fan of garlic spray. Garlic is not just good at keeping the aphids away, it's wonderful as a tonic for the plant as it's high in sulphur and also helps against mildew.'

Chelsea Flower Show is only a couple of weeks away and the Herb Farm about to have an Open Weekend when customers have a chance to buy on site, and indeed, to meet Jekka. The mountain of compost in the background frames tall angelica plants, destined for the show. Vibrantly green thymes are in full bud. There's a myrtle hedge for Chelsea. I

see a beautiful pomegranate and sneak in a question about my own rather less healthy pomegranate. 'Oh, they'll flower in this country, they don't mind the cold weather but you won't have any fruits.' Jekka talks about Hampton Court. She's had Best in Show a couple of years running. 'Chelsea's great but Best in Show means you've beaten the orchids and roses. It's just wonderful.' A well-deserved accolade I think for someone who is a doyenne at her game and, incidentally, likes to add a little humour into her plant world. We pass a pot of Jekka's Slip Up, a cross between an oxslip and a cowslip. 'The seeds seem to have got muddled.' Like rose growers, there's always something new, in this case an oregano, Jekka's Little Beauty. This is *Origanum dictamnus* (Cretan Oregano) crossed with *Origanum rotunda folium*, 'Kent Beauty'.

From basil to borage, mint to horseradish, fennel to rosemary, all can be ordered from the farm either by email or telephone. The farm is open to the public on only four weekends a year but for those living within driving distance, orders can be left outside the nursery for collection.

JONATHAN CRUMP

Standish Park Farm, Oxlynch, Stonehouse, Gloucestershire GL10 3DG
Tel: 01453 821486

The story of Old Gloucester cattle wears the mantle of an agricultural romance. Their existence was well documented in the late eighteenth century although some say records went back to the Domesday Book. The cattle were long time native to the Cotswolds and the Severn Vale, beautiful fine-horned animals, deep polished mahogany in colour with a white stripe running down the back, extending down the tail, over the udders and along the underbelly – and known as finchbacks. Owing to disease, numbers began to decline and Longhorns began to replace them. Foot-and-mouth took a further toll in the early twentieth century and by 1930, only 142 animals remained. Inbreeding produced yet more problems. In a nutshell, by 1966, Wick Court in Arlingham in the Vale of Berkeley became the last stronghold. The Misses Ella and Alex, the redoubtable Dowdeswell sisters, owned this mediaeval mansion, but by 1972 could no longer manage the farm and the herd was divided and sold. Move forward to the 1980s when a young Jonathan Crump, at that time a boy living in Surrey, had read about Wick Court and was fascinated by the Dowdeswells and their Gloucester cows. He met and was interviewed by the board of the charitable trust that were trying to restore the house and farm. Jonathan saw both the potential and the magic of the Vale of Berkeley on the banks of the Severn, flanked by the Forest of Dean on one side and the Cotswolds on the other. In 1992 he moved to Wick Court to care for his new purchase, five Old Gloucesters – two cows and three heifers, and to start farming in conjunction with the current project running there – Farms for City Children.

During his time at Wick Court, Jonathan aimed to return the land to the traditional rhythm of life as practised over many decades in the Vale of Berkeley, with apple orchards producing apples for cider whilst Gloucester Old Spot pigs grazed the orchards and munched the windfall fruits. The Old Gloucester cows provided the milk for his Double and Single Gloucester cheeses, the whey further enriching the pigs' diet. Like many good things that seem ideal, there was a hiccup. City children were staying on the farm, the cows had horns and nerves started to jangle in the Health and Safety office.

Jonathan and his herd moved at the beginning of 2009 to a new premises, together with a couple of Kerry cows and the Old Spot pigs. The permanent pasture on which the animals graze, including the more recent addition of a mixed herd of Cotswold and Jacobs sheep that he's had since he was twelve, is a sheltered bowl on the edge of the Severn Vale, fringed by woodland in the care of the National Trust. Stephen Morris likened Jonathan to Dr Doolittle. As we talked and Stephen photographed, animals wandered in and out of the barn. Rhubarb, a cow with a dislike of the cold north easterly that was blowing, sauntered in for a mouthful of hay; piglets not yet weaned but unwilling to miss out on a good party, gazed at the ewe whose lamb we held. Nearby a couple of Tamworths were confined to barracks, having behaved true to form and escaped the previous day.

But this is digressing from the serious farming that takes place, with sustainability always in its sights. Hay for the cattle is produced on the farm. Jonathan neither makes nor feeds silage, feeling it is no good for wildlife and that it can also taint the milk. Hay, he thinks, is much better for flowers and insects. His pork and lamb are sold locally but his main farming emphasis is on the production of Double and Single Gloucester cheese, using the milk from the Old Gloucester cows.

The dairy is newly converted from an old shed, as is the milking parlour and the latter is probably the only one of its type over the last 50 years to be installed and returned to the system of traditional yokes by which to tether the cattle during milking. The cattle are small by modern-day standards and the milk yield is much lower, but high protein and small fat globules give quality and individuality to the cheese. Some Single Gloucester incorporates half-skimmed milk but Jonathan uses full-cream milk with a maturing time of a couple of months. The Double Gloucester with its higher acidity must mature for longer and is ultimately a richer cheese. They are both superb, the milk from the cattle giving them a unique identity and quality.

Cheeses are available from Stroud Farmers' Market, Paxton and Whitfield, Hania Cheese in Stroud,* Chandos Delicatessens in Bristol, Puddleditch Farm Shop on the A38,* Pound Farm Shop, Waddon and William's Kitchen in Nailsworth.*

* See pages 126 to 127

Blossom's contribution to world health

A little more about Old Gloucester cows

Edward Jenner (1749-1823), the founding father of immunology, embarked on his medical career at the end of the eighteenth century in Berkeley, Gloucestershire. Although relatively rare, cowpox had been reported in the area. In 1796, a milkmaid named Sarah Nelmes contracted it from an Old Gloucester cow called Blossom, through a scratch on her hand. Jenner, long believing cowpox could offer protection against smallpox, wanted to test his thesis. To do this he needed fluid from the sore on her hand in order to infect someone else – and chose James Phipps, the eight-year-old son of his gardener whom he knew to be fit and with no history of smallpox. On 14 May 1796, Jenner made a scratch on the boy's arm and rubbed it with the infected liquid. Four days later the boy developed two cowpox pustules and a light fever that quickly subsided. On 1st July 1796 Edward Jenner inoculated the boy with the deadly smallpox virus but the lad remained healthy – there was no illness, the cowpox had immunized him against the killer disease and ultimately – in 1980 – Jenner's goal would be achieved, the total eradication of smallpox.

The Edward Jenner Museum and Conference Centre, Church Lane, Berkeley, Gloucestershire, GL13 9BN. Tel: 01453 810631 www.jennermuseum.com

OLD SODBURY LAMB

Andy and Sarah Williams, 6 Church Lane, Old Sodbury, South Gloucestershire BS37 6NB
Tel: 01454 323416 Mob: 07730 580748

In South Gloucestershire and barely a shake of a lamb's tail from Old Sodbury, Andy Williams shepherds a flock of Swaledale Blue Face Leicester sheep, their grazing ground bordering on the Cotswold Way, well loved by hikers. It has always seemed to me that sheep dogs are highly intelligent, just so with Andy's dog, Tess – until of course you think that every dog's dream is to be allowed to chase sheep – and the fortunate Tess does it with her master's blessing, consummate skill and a lolloping grin. It's impressive to see. Their choice of breed combines the hardy hill sheep with a lowland variety for the meat quality, the latter very apparent when you taste Andy Williams' lamb.

There is nothing hurried about the lives of these animals. The rams go in with the flock in about October so the Williams' lambing season is March, by which time they hope the hardest part of the winter is over. At present the lambing pens are housed in a poly-tunnel, a shivery place on a cold night but the sheep are very much a family business and Andy's wife Sarah and their two sons frequently leave their comfortable beds, particularly during lambing. The survival rate is very high with maybe the occasional hungry fox helping himself. Cold can be a problem if the lambs are not on their feet and feeding quickly enough, but Andy says he's amazed how fast they recover once they're warmed up and begin to drink the ewe's milk. Their lives thereafter are focussed on unhurried grazing, entirely on permanent pasture, until time of slaughter. The butchery is done in Chipping Sodbury at Artingstalls Family Butchers where the meat is also on sale.

In tandem with the sheep, Andy runs a livestock haulage business, transporting for local farmers to local markets. He also fires up something he calls The Rocket, a wood-burning-fired mobile oven that goes with him to food festivals and catering events and where the family sell their home-produced sausages and lamb burgers.

Andy Williams' lamb is on sale at Chipping Sodbury Farmers' Market, Whiteladies Road Farmers' Market in Bristol, at the University of the West of England Local Produce Market in Bristol or by telephone.

JESS'S LADIES ORGANIC MILK

Jess Vaughan, Hardwicke Farm, Haywick Lane, Hardwicke, Gloucestershire GL2 3QE
Tel: 01452 720343 Email: info@theladiesorganicmilk.co.uk www.theladiesorganicmilk.co.uk

Outside the farmhouse door a small cat curled itself into a large dog's food bowl to sleep in a shaft of sunlight. Three generations of Vaughans have lived in the farmhouse and run Hardwicke Farm; this was where Jess's father Mike grew up, farming with his father John. Jess too spent her childhood here and after studying Agriculture at Aberystwyth University, joined her father in 2002 to help look after the eighty-strong herd of Hardwicke Friesians. A couple of years before Jess's return, Mike Vaughan had secured organic status for their traditionally managed farmland with its pastures, woodland, ancient oaks and hedgerows, close to the Gloucester and Sharpness Canal.

The Hardwicke Friesian herd are deep-bodied predominantly black cows, all descendants of the first four animals brought to the farm by Jess's grandfather, hence earning the appellation of The Hardwicke Herd. Walking out to meet these gentle beasts, Jess described each by name, chatting about their idiosyncrasies and life history. The health and welfare of the animals is of paramount importance to the Vaughans and the superb quality of the milk and cream, seen as a natural conclusion of good treatment. The cows are well rested before calving and at no stage is their milk production pushed. Life is as stress-free as possible for the herd, affectionately known to the family and now to their customers as The Ladies.

To produce healthy animals and good milk, pasture and silage must be up to scratch. Jess's clarion call is 'we love clover', in other words, the Vaughans follow the timeless rule of rotation of crops, using clover to fix nitrogen into the soil to feed cereal crops, negating the use of fertilizers, herbicides and pesticides. She describes the drone of the bees working on the red clover flowers on a summer's day and the wildlife on the canal banks and in the woodland. Swallows, woodpeckers, hares and rabbits are amongst their local residents – and seven barn owls, one of which lives in the hollow oak and of which they are particularly proud. The family feel it's proof of their harmonious farming.

Hardwicke Farm produced a masterful stroke when the Vaughans began to bottle their own milk in 2006, branded as Jess's Ladies Organic Farm Milk. Conventional supermarket-style labels were imaginatively replaced with labels using a floral cottage wallpaper background, hung with various portraits of Jess with her Ladies, each according to the type of milk. As Jess said, 'it achieved everything we wished to convey.' Certainly the milk is the most delicious I've drunk since childhood. 'The main reason,' says Jess, 'is the animals' life style, forage and our attention to detail at all levels, but additionally our milk is not homogenised, a technique used to give milk a longer shelf life.' Once upon a time milk left on the doorstep would separate into a creamy couple of inches on the top with the thinner milk below; all and sundry including garden birds who pecked their way through the milk bottle tops, vied for that creamy bit. It doesn't happen any more because homogenising, pushing the milk through a minute sieve at speed irreversibly fractures the milk's molecular structure, hence no creamy top. Recent Danish research has shown these tiny fat particles can sometimes pass into the blood stream after homogenisation and cause dairy allergies, but from a marketing point of view of course, the milk has a longer shelf life and doesn't absorb smell.

Jess's Ladies dairy sales are to farm shops, coffee shops, delicatessens and restaurants. Their list included semi-skimmed, skimmed whole milk, wonderful cream, a natural creamy yoghurt, and of course the great favourite, the unique Breakfast Milk. Whereas whole milk must be below 3.9% fat, cows naturally produce milk with 4.5% fat – that's Jess's Ladies Breakfast Milk. 'It's been a sharp learning curve,' says Jess. Five a.m. in the milking parlour may be a challenge but she has already proved her skills by winning two gold medals in The Great Taste Awards in 2008, the first time any milk has achieved such an accolade – and well worth a fanfare on the milk churns.

You can find Jess at Stroud Farmers' Market on a Saturday.

SELSLEY HERB AND SPICE COMPANY

Paul Hunt, Selsley Herb and Spice Company, Wimberley Mills, Brimscombe, Stroud, Gloucestershire GL5 2TH
Tel: 01453 882528 Email: info@selsleyherbandspice.com www.selsleyherbandspice.com

Selsley Herb and Spice Company is perhaps slightly ambiguous in terms of what the business does today, but the name goes back to the origins of the company, started by a couple in the mid-eighties who set up a herb farm and developed a food product range around their herbs, rather than selling them solo. Paul Hunt took over the company a couple of years ago and strives to keep within the parameters of the original company. Marmalades including Lavender, Ginger, Cardamom and a savoury Red Onion that's excellent with goat cheese were amongst the original products; also vinegars and oils incorporating fresh pasteurised herbs. Everything is made in Brimscombe, and Paul's wife Natalie is the proud creator of their most popular line today, Tomato, Chilli and Roasted Garlic Chutney. Other unusual chutneys include Fennel, Celery and Cucumber and Beetroot and Blueberry. Mustards come under their umbrella including grained mustard and a local speciality, Tewkesbury, which incorporates horseradish and is often used in the traditional Gloucestershire cheese and ale recipe.[1] Tewskesbury mustard dates at least as far back as the sixteenth century as Shakespeare gives it a mention in Henry IV when Falstaff says 'his wit was as thick as Tewkesbury mustard.' Black Olive mustard is another Selsley favourite. Paul makes delicious dessert syrups such as ginger and vanilla. He claims to no longer notice the heady aromas that waft around his premises but it's a haven of good smells, thanks not least to the mulling syrup for wine, a heady combination of cinnamon, nutmeg, orange and cloves. Remember ginger beer plants? He produces those too, all ready to take away and fire up a home brew.

Selsley Herb and Spice Company produce is sold at Stroud, Swindon, Gloucester and Stow-on-the-Wold Farmers' Markets and in several delicatessens and shops including Frocester Fayre Farm Shop.[2]

1 See recipe on page 80
2 See Frocester Fayre entry on page 37

SEVERN AND WYE SMOKERY

Richard Cook, Severn and Wye Smokery, Chaxhill, Westbury-on-Severn, Gloucestershire GL14 1QW
Tel: 01452 760190 Email: info@severnandwye.co.uk www.severnandwye.co.uk

For a smoked eel aficionado, the Severn and Wye Smokery, only yards from the great river, was a delectable introduction occasioned by Marco Pierre White who, with his Mr Ishi in tow, was to be seen enthusing about the Smokery's eel on his television programme in which he sought out Britain's favourite foods. Marco and Mr Ishi were correct; the eel is superb. The skipper of the fish smokery, Richard Cook, is a man who knows a lot about local terrain, about eel fishing and about fish in general – his father still fishes on the river.

On the subject of eel, no-one disputes the silver eels are endangered but Richard Cook views the scarcity of elvers – the young eels – more as a result of anti-flood installations in the river than of over fishing or excessive export. He explains the divide of local spoils used to be that the gentry took the salmon, leaving the elver fishing as the right of the poorer people of Gloucester, Lydney and surrounds, enabling the latter to enjoy this rich protein during the season. 'But the parameters changed. Elvers and eels became recognized as a delicacy and the price went up. Simultaneously, the elvers enter the river as fragile fry having travelled from the Sargasso Sea, and they are completely controlled by the tidal influence. The tide sweeps them up the river, theoretically into ditches, dykes and ponds. Every tributary threatening a flood risk to development is now shut off by a clapper gate so although we have huge flood plains, it's a struggle for the fish to access their natural habitat. Local clappers force the fish further and further up the river as far as Tewksbury Weir. In other words, the main arteries to the Severn are shut off so the eels no longer have easy access to their natural habitat.'

However, the Severn Smokery deals right across the fishy spectrum. Salmon, wild and farmed, herring, cod – you name it, they smoke it, thirty-five tonnes of fish a week. But smoking is only part of the business. We talked about the improved quality of farmed salmon. 'The Norwegians control the industry, be under no illusions, but this is because they're very good at it.' Richard Cook's retail shop, run by his wife Shirley, has a counter as stacked with fat, fresh, gleaming fish as I've ever seen, worthy of a special expedition. I asked him what his favourite fish dish was: 'early wild salmon poached with bay leaf and onion – and eaten cold. Or maybe a pan-fried sea bass with crispy skin.'

This is a seven-days-a-week industry. Much of their local fish comes from Wales, Swansea and Burry Port. Richard is a wise enough man to have a Welsh intermediary who buys from the day boats and delivers nightly to the smokery. 'An Englishman can't buy direct from a Welshman, unless they've just won the rugby!' Richard describes himself and his business as 'the wholesalers' wholesaler'; he buys with panache and sells not only retail but also to the trade as far afield as Dubai, Abu Dhabi, Greece, Italy and Mauritius. People travel to see him, Marco Pierre White in March and Gordon Ramsay in May last year.

At present no water is discharged from the Smokery; rather it's retained for irrigation; all polystyrene boxes are

recycled and nothing goes to the tip. There is a scheme afoot, pending planning permission, to use a wind turbine: 'wind is something we have plenty of – and it's free.' And to help local school children focus on their environment, the business is funding a fish tank in every primary school in the area where the children can follow the hatching of fish fry and learn a little of the ways of the river for themselves. Reforestation, the planting of big traditional trees like oak, beech and ash are also on the agenda.

The shop is open from Monday-Friday, 9.00am-6.00pm: Saturdays, 9.00am-5.00pm.

SIMON WEAVER

Cotswold Organic Dairy, Kirkham Farm, Upper Slaughter, Gloucestershire GL54 2JS
Tel: 01451 870852 Email: info@turnstonefarming.co.uk www.simonweaver.net

As dairy farmers in the heart of glorious Gloucestershire countryside, when prices for organic milk plummeted, Simon and Carol Weaver switched to cheese making and to seeing their business progress from meadow to market – from milking their herd of 185 Friesian cows to their current production of four different styles of cheese. They view Friesians as the best choice for the dairy herd as the breed give good butter fats for the Weavers' style of organic cheeses. Carol went to Germany and Holland to tap into the basics of cheese making, since when the Weavers have experimented and developed their own different style. Whilst anxious to listen to their customers, Simon says he and Carol have learned over time to stick to what they themselves like, rather than veering off in too many directions on too many whims. Their ethos is firmly based on connecting their local landscape with the food it creates, 'our cheeses reflect our clean fresh pastures that produce the milk.'

Cheeses are made in small moulds; they pass through a very hot room where the draining process takes place, bugs are destroyed and the cheeses turned several times to prevent the bottoms becoming soggy: ultimately this helps with even ripening. It's a classic procedure for making young, soft cheese. After a week in the ripening room, they move on to be wrapped and labelled and to mature for a further week or two before hitting the market.

The present collection are their prize-winning Cotswold Brie, Cotswold Blue which is a blue-veined version of the Brie, Herb Cheese with fresh herbs incorporated while the cheese is still in the vat – and a Smoked Cheese, made on the farm but organically smoked in Shropshire. Simon's recommendation is that all the cheeses are eaten at room temperature; he's particularly sold on the combination of fresh pear with blue cheese, 'blue cheeses are great with a little sweetness.' It's well worth looking at their excellent website for further recipe ideas.

The farm sells from the door; they are always open Monday-Friday 9.00am–5.00pm. Farmers' Markets include Stroud, Banbury, Chipping Norton, Stow-on-the-Wold, Deddington, Bourton-on-the-Water, Oxford and Mosely. All good shops locally sell the cheese, including Mabys Deli in Stow-on-the-Wold. Sainsburys stock the little 50g Bries.

DIANA SMART

Old Ley Court, Chapel Lane, Birdwood, Churcham, Gloucestershire GL2 8AR
Tel: 01452 750225 www.smartsgloucestercheese.com

Diana Smart's greeting in the farmyard included a pertinent question, 'had I seen *The Forester* this week?' She was well amused to be a star in her local paper, pictured with an indie pop group, The Macabees. 'I don't know what an indie group is but they were doing a video about the man who'd won the Gloucester cheese rolling contest for several years and the group wanted to see where the cheese was made. They bought a cheese and left rolling it down the drive: they were lovely lads.' Diana Smart has been making cheese for twenty-two years; she began when she was 60-years-old. The Macabees had made an educated choice in their venerable cheese tutor, particularly as Diana's cheeses are used every year for this idiosyncratic event that takes place on Cooper's Hill in Brockworth. The cheeses can apparently reach speeds of up to 70 miles an hour.

Mrs Smart and her husband were farmers and for many years did a milk round in Gloucester selling unpasteurized milk. 'I used to buy in some cheese to sell on the round. People wanted mild cheddar, but I wouldn't have it on my van as I regard it as an insult to cheese. I persuaded them to try something with more flavour. I used to make lots of yoghurt for the milk round and we did unpasteurized double cream that you could stand a spoon up in. I wanted to make cheese but didn't know anything about it. Luckily there was a business advertised in the local press and the chap, John Crisp, who was selling it was willing to teach me, so of course I was thrilled to bits. When he said he made Double Gloucester, I said, oh, I don't want to make that rubbish. You see, I'd only ever tasted it in supermarkets. He gave me a bit of what he'd made six months previously and I said, oh boy, if I can make it like that I do want to make Double Gloucester. So we bought the business!' The business has a mixed herd of Holstein, Brown Swiss and Old Gloucesters – the latter are obligatory amongst a herd in order to make Single Gloucester cheese which has a PDO (Protected Derivation of Origin) status. The Brown Swiss are Diana's favourites, 'because they're beautiful, they're quiet and they give lots of milk. They look almost like big Jerseys with a lovely soft colour and white bits around their noses.'

The farm makes cheeses a couple of days a week, when visitors are welcome to see the process, alternating between Single and Double Gloucester. Today's cheese curds had reached the stage of milling and salting, a necessary part of the procedure for Double Gloucester cheese. Diana's son Rod and helper Gary assembled the Victorian hand-mill, a piece of equipment remarkable for its simplicity, pristine condition despite its years – and looking rather like a mangle with teeth, alternatively an instrument of torture. Gary peeled off the layers of partially-made curded cheese and fed them into the mill while Rod turned its handle; the shredded curds tumbled back into the bath ready to be salted and finally packed into moulds prior to pressing and maturation, in the case of Double Gloucester, for six months. The cheeses are pressed initially in beautiful cast-iron Victorian cheese presses.

We moved to the cheese store to taste some of her cheeses and began discussing Patrick Rance, author of *The Great British Cheese Book*. 'Patrick once said to me, you can't mature a Single Gloucester Cheese. We had some Single Gloucester that had been pushed to the back of the shelf and forgotten about. We took it out and tasted it and it was rather good, so we kept it for about another year and decided it was superb so I took it to a specialist cheese show that Patrick was attending and everybody was raving about it. I gave him a little bit and he said; that's a mature Single Gloucester. That's all he said. I was tickled about that! The cheese is called Harefield and it's my answer to Parmesan. When my son died 14 years ago I said I was going to make another batch of Harefield and that will prove that I'll keep going for another two years. It's been my salvation.' The Harefield is a hard cheese with an intense nutty flavour and sold by Diana only in the Farmers' Markets or directly from the farm. As tradition dictates in Gloucestershire, the whey from the cheese-making is fed to Diana's Gloucester Old Spot pigs.

Telephone first, but on Tuesdays and Thursdays, cheese-making days, she sells her cheese from the door, also thick rashers of Old Spot bacon and wonderful sausages. Alternatively Diana Smart is at Lydney, Cheltenham, Usk, St Briavels and Monmouth Farmers' Markets. Her cheeses are sold at Neals Yard, Covent Garden, Hunter and Todd Newnham-on-Severn and the Severn and Wye Smokery in Chaxhill.

THE ULEY BREWERY

Chas Wright, Uley Brewery Ltd, The Old Brewery, 31 The Street, Uley, Gloucestershire GL11 5TP
Tel: 01453 860120 Email: chas@uleybrewery.com www.uleybrewery.com

One might question how the hamlet of Uley could have justified thirteen beer houses in the village in 1840. The answer was that at the time, there were numerous woollen mills in the area. Working in the mills was tiring and thirsty work so in 1833 Mr Samuel Price set about quenching thirsts and building a brewery into the hillside, flanking it with its own maltings, stable and coach house where the dray horses were kept. A seventeenth-century weaver's house still stands on the corner of the complex. To make a good brew there must also be a source of good water; the busy stream beside the brewery percolates through Cotswold limestone, providing hard spring water ideal for brewing. Such is the reputation of the water that the Roman invaders made an altar in their temple just north of the brewery, both to the stream and to the water gods.

The dray horses may have gone and the Maris Otter malted barley be shipped from Tuckers Maltings in Devon, but the brewing team at Uley, led by the larger-than-life Mr Chas Wright, provide a timeless air to the place and an ale so good that beer specialist and writer Roger Protz lists Uley ale as one of the three hundred beers to drink before you die! In a sunny spot in the yard the smell of warm barley husks pervades; they've been heaped on a cart and designated as the next meal for a few Gloucester Old Spot pigs. That particular load of malted barley husks had just done its job by providing fermentable sugars that were extracted in the mash tun in the first stage of brewing, leaving behind a liquid called wort, now awaiting the addition of the all-important hops.

Back inside the brewery there was a bit of excitement going on. The wort had been boiled up in the copper and Ken Lush, head brewer, was about to open the lid. 'It's a wonderful moment when the hops go in,' said Ken. And so it was. First saltiness, then steamy bittersweet herbaceous smells billowed from the copper as the hops hit the hot wort. The hops are from over the county border in Herefordshire; Goldings and Fuggles for rounded English-style flavour and sometimes the addition of a bittering hop called Pilgrim. Ken added that craft brewing was really a euphemism for doing everything by hand. The Boss construed it as meaning that Ken and Stu-the-Brew could time pub visits to perfection between critical moments in the brewery. The trick it seems is that fermenting vessels are all-important in the brewing game and the ratio of the exposed surfaces governs the rate of fermentation; the skill of the small brewer is that he can control that fermentation very accurately.

Outside, the Gloucester Old Spot weather vane above the brewery veered a little in the breeze and we fell into conversation about pubs. Chas said that he only sold his ales into genuine free trade pubs. The beer at Uley is all in cask, 'a proper brewery doesn't need to bottle beer – it just spoils good beer!' In fact as Chas Wright pointed out, a cask of ale contains the equivalent of something like three hundred cans, the cans adding to the cost of the beer and creating recycling problems. Amongst their regular beers are Uley Bitter, Old Spot,

Hogshead, Pig's Ear, Old Ric – and Laurie Lee Bitter. The story of the latter ran thus. Laurie Lee's village of Slad is over the hill and Chas Wright had promised to name a beer after him when he died. Prompted to keep to his word by Laurie Lee's widow, they made the beer, poured a pint over the grave, which didn't wake him up, so the beer went on draught in the Woolpack in Slad, Laurie Lee's favourite pub – an establishment described by Jody Veale, another of the Uley brewing team, as a donkey-jacket or dinner-jacket place. Old Ric is the house beer for The Old Spot pub in nearby Dursley, voted pub of the year in 2008 and the beer named after its late owner, Ric Sainty. Brewing does not get better or more traditional than this.

THREE CHOIRS VINEYARD

Newent, Gloucestershire GL18 1LS
Tel: 01531 890223 Email: info@threechoirs.com www.threechoirs.com

To arrive at Three Choirs Vineyard is a little similar to driving into some of the well-tended vineyards in the Napa and Sonoma Valleys in California: except that here in Gloucestershire the vineyard seems more accessible, prices less scary and things are not over manicured. The seventy-five-acre vineyard takes its name from playing host to the Three Choirs Festival from Gloucester, Worcester and Hereford cathedrals. Early in the seventies it was a fruit farm, bought by Alan Mackechnie and planted with half an acre of vines as an experiment. It ticked over until the early nineties when John Oldacre bought into the business; thereafter the turnaround began from farm to serious vineyard. Around this time Tom Shaw joined the company, bringing his expertise in farming and wine-making from Australia.

Tom Shaw is clear about their objectives. Three Choirs try to straddle a middle ground between an operating vineyard and a tourist attraction, but do not want to be snobby about their wines. Wines should be for pleasure and not too academic and Tom certainly doesn't want to copy other people's style just to toe the line. After all, he says, the French don't do it. They make and blend their wines according to the harvest.
In 2008, Three Choirs won the Oscar of the English wine world, the Gore Browne Trophy for their Siegerebbe 2006 – and it was an immediate sell-out. 2009 saw further success

with their single varietal Siegerebbe 2007, again a winner in the English and Welsh Wine of the Year contest. The Siegerebbe grape has a propensity for early ripening, the wine is an aromatic white, well in line with the way we like to think of our English wines. Their winemaker, Martin Fowke, winner of the McAlpine 'Best Winemaker' 2008 award, also makes wines for about thirty other vineyards.

I asked Tom Shaw about his favourite wines. 'The Fume, that's our Seyval Blanc aged in new French or American oak – using American oak gives the wine a little more sweetness, a touch more vanilla. Seyval is quite a bland grape so it takes oak well and it's easy to grow in this climate.' Tom likes the wine when it's young and crisp but customers tend to like it a little older. Bacchus too ages well, and Siegerebbe, but not much more than eight years: there are older wines in their cellars but these are more for novelty value. A surprising twenty per cent of the vineyard is dedicated to red wine production, Pinot Noir for sparkling wines, or sometimes they sell it as a single grape variety if the mood takes them. And there's Rondo, Regent and Triomphe d'Alsace.

Just occasionally, when conditions are right, the vineyard produces a late harvest or more rarely a noble harvest when grapes develop the beginnings of botrytis and can subsequently be made into delicious dessert wines. Three Choirs have a little micro-brewery on site where they brew, amongst others, a beer called Dick Whittington in honour of the eponymous Mr Whittington, locally born.

Once the harvest is over, pruning begins at the end of November when the leaves have dropped. Cuttings are chopped and go back into the ground whilst lanes between the vines are kept permanently grassed to help hold the soil in place. Welsh mountains to the west, the Malverns to the north and the Cotswolds to the east, this splendid vineyard also has lodges where guests can stay and commune with Bacchus or the odd hedgehog on a late-night foray; accommodation runs to eleven bedrooms and a restaurant. I dashed into the shop before leaving and bought a bottle of their delicious Premium Selection Rosé.

Shop open:
Sunday-Thursday 9.00am-5.00pm;
Friday and Saturday 9.00am-7.00pm.

ST ANNE'S VINEYARD

David and Paula Jenkins, Oxenhall, Near Newent, Gloucestershire GL18 1RW
Tel: 01989 720313 Email: david@stannesvineyard.fsnet.co.uk   www.stannesvineyard.com

There's no such thing as a quiet time of year if you're in the business of making both grape and fruit wines. In addition to grape wine, David and Paula Jenkins make damson, gooseberry, strawberry, crab apple, cherry, cowslip, honeysuckle – and more besides. Fruit wines need some grape juice behind them to give them oomph, so on the Jenkinses' two and a half acres of land they also grow varieties of grapes efficiently productive in this country such as Madeleine Angevine, Seyval Blanc, Triomphe and several others. About 30 per cent of the vineyard production is used to make their grape wine, the rest is down to fruit. Only on reading the impressive list does it become apparent this means picking quantities of fruit and flowers, all of which they try to do as locally as possible and several varieties of which they grow themselves including the mysterious Josterberry that evolves into a dusty pink wine. Josterberry is a cross between gooseberry and blackcurrant, its flavour as enigmatic to pinpoint as the plant itself. Although the wine is dry, it throws off a smell a little like rosehips. Fruit wines they may be, but several come with a good thwack of alcohol, some as high as 14.5° vol and all are reasonably priced at around £5.

It seems a bold venture for a couple who had previously lived in Italy and who run this enterprise in tandem with other work. But Italy, says Paula, was where everyone with a garden grew a few vines and made a little wine and this was their inspiration. When they returned to England, the house and the vineyard – planted initially in 1979 – were for sale so the Jenkinses took the plunge. In addition to fruit wines, St Anne's also sells fortified wines and a sparkling wine, made for them by Three Choirs Vineyard.

St Anne's Vineyard shop is open at weekends in winter from 11.00am-5.00pm. Summer opening hours: Wednesday-Friday 2.00pm-6.00pm; Saturdays, Sundays and Bank Holidays 11.00am-6.00pm.

Farmers' Markets: Gloucester, Cheltenham, Stroud, Leominster, Hereford, Lydney, Pershore and Queen's Park in London.

The Recipes

Gloucestershire has good arable land and is traditionally a dairy county with rich grasslands attributable to the influence of the Severn. Falling milk prices a year or so ago led more farmers to diversify, some to cheese making and the county's cheeses are exceptionally good. Traditionally Gloucester Old Spot pigs, synonymous with the county, were fed the whey from the cheese making and in the autumn munched the fallen orchard fruits. The recipes in the book, although not necessarily traditional, reflect where possible what grows readily on the land or what will, one hopes, enhance that local produce.

Serves 4 to 6

A steamer for vegetables is great news because the vegetables taste better and the remaining water in the pan after steaming makes a good basic stock for soups. This recipe for a winter warmer is cooked entirely in a steamer.

Top of the steamer
400g (14oz) celeriac, peeled weight
1 medium potato, peeled
1 large onion, peeled

Bottom of the steamer
1 carrot, peeled
1 bay leaf
2 thyme sprigs
½ lemon
1 chicken stock cube
1½ litres (2¾ pints) water

To finish the soup
salt, pepper and celery salt (or nutmeg)
single cream
2 tbsp chopped chives or parsley

1 Cut all the peeled vegetables into chunks. Put the celeriac, potato and onion into the top half of the steamer and the carrot, bay leaf, thyme, half lemon, stock cube and water in the bottom part. Steam until the celeriac, potato and onion are cooked.

2 Spoon the thyme, lemon and bay leaf from the water and discard. Blend the contents from the top half and bottom half of the steamer together, add salt, pepper and 1 level teaspoonful of celery salt or a good grating of nutmeg. Stir in the cream and chopped chives and serve immediately.

Enough for 4 to 6 pieces of toast

A traditional Gloucestershire recipe and the county's answer to Welsh rarebit. This is the sort of stuff for fireside eating when conversation's good and the stomach's rumbling.

200g (7oz) Double or Single Gloucester cheese

Tewkesbury mustard

good ale

fresh bread

1 Slice the cheese fairly thinly, place in a baking dish and spread with Tewkesbury mustard. Cover the cheese with a little ale and bake in a medium oven until the mixture bubbles.

2 Toast thick slices of bread, splash with ale and pour the cheese mixture over the top. An accompanying pint is essential.

Serves 4

This must be the quickest supper dish ever – but that's once the onion marmalade has been made. The marmalade keeps well in the fridge and is delicious with hot or cold meats as well as goat cheese and cheddar.

Goat cheese

8 sheets filo pastry

25g (1oz) melted butter

4 small medium or strong goat cheeses

Pre-heat oven to 220°C (425°F) gas mark 7

1 Using two sheets of filo pastry for each cheese, wrap the cheeses in loose parcels, painting the outside of the pastry with the melted butter as you wrap. Place on a baking tray and into the oven for 8-10 minutes until the filo is crisp and golden.

Serve with onion marmalade and a rocket and herb salad.

Red onion marmalade

3 red onions

3 tbsp olive oil

175ml (6 fl oz) red wine

125ml (4 fl oz) red wine vinegar

115g (4oz) soft muscovado sugar

salt and pepper

1 Peel and thinly slice the onions and sauté gently in the oil until soft. Add the remaining ingredients and simmer, uncovered, for about an hour, stirring from time to time.

2 Store in the fridge when cold: keeps for two to three weeks.

Roast Beetroot With Sea Salt and Rosemary

Enough for 4 to 6 pieces of toast

David Wilson, the farm manager from The Duchy Home Farm and a man who likes beetroot, gave me this tip. Trim and wash the beetroot, wrap individually in tinfoil with a little sea salt and a sprig of rosemary and roast in a medium oven (below the joint), for a couple of hours.

The flavour is excellent and it's a fine vegetable with meat. If there are any cooked beetroots left over, I like them diced and mixed with walnut oil, lemon juice and salt and pepper.

Serves 6

Courgette pudding is a variation on Yorkshire pudding-cum-tarte tatin, in other words, an upside-down pudding – and it's easiest made in a large tarte tatin tin. Turn it out and eat while still warm, either as a starter or light lunch – or in your fingers with a glass of wine.

2 tbsp sunflower oil

2-3 courgettes

75g (2¾ oz) plain flour

salt and pepper

1 egg

75ml (3 fl oz) milk

50ml (2 fl oz) cold water

50g (1¾ oz) finely grated Double Gloucester cheese

1 tsp finely chopped basil

Pre-heat the oven to 220ºC (425ºF) gas mark 7

1 Line the tin with baking parchment. Pour the oil into the bottom of the baking tin and make sure the edges too are well oiled. Slice the courgettes and arrange over the base of the tin.

2 Sift the flour and a little salt and pepper into a bowl and make a well in the centre. Whisk the egg, milk and water together and add gradually to the flour, beating constantly. Add the cheese and basil and give a final whisk.

3 Put the courgettes in the oven for 5 minutes until the fat is sizzling. Pour the batter over the courgettes and bake for a further 25 minutes, until golden and firm to touch.
Turn out onto a cake rack.

Makes 6-8 pies

Try as I may – Googling, enquiries within The Guild of Food Writers, asking food lovers both English and American – I cannot tell you the provenance of Hommity Pies, only that their base ingredients are potatoes, onion, garlic and cheese, more usually Cheddar. What is certain is that they are simple and delicious, particularly when made with Double Gloucester cheese.

Pastry

    150g (5½ oz) plain flour

    75g (2¾ oz) butter

    pinch salt

    iced water

Filling

    250g (9 oz) cooked potato – a waxy variety

    1 medium onion

    2-3 garlic cloves

    200g (7 oz) button mushrooms

    1 tbsp sunflower oil

    2 tbsp fresh chopped parsley

    1 tbsp Worcestershire sauce

    100g (3½ oz) Double Gloucester cheese, finely grated

    salt and pepper

    2 tbsp double cream

Pre-heat the oven to 190°C (375°F) gas mark 5.
Use either little individual quiche tins or a tray for baking little cakes or tarts.

⌉ Make the pastry. Lightly oil the tart or cake tins and line with pastry.

2 Peel and finely chop the onion and garlic; chop the mushrooms into quarters. Heat the oil in a frying pan and soften the onion, add the garlic and mushrooms and cook for a further minute or two. Let it cool for 5 minutes before adding to the other ingredients.

3 Dice the potatoes into a large bowl; add the chopped parsley, cheese and Worcestershire Sauce and finally the onion and mushroom mixture. Fold the ingredients together and spoon into the pastry cases. Trickle a little cream over each. Bake for 25 minutes and serve warm or cold.

Makes about 6 jars

Medlars are unprepossessing little fruits, like tiny russet apples and when cut in half they resemble an apple in cross section. To enjoy a raw medlar, the fruit must be ripe, that's to say it looks brown and mushy – in medlar-speak, bletted. Cut in half and scoop out the flesh. Medlar jelly has the sharpness and cut of crab apple, but more flavour and it's perfect with meats such as lamb and pork or eaten by the spoonful on fresh bread or little pancakes with cream. There are plenty growing within the county and they are around at the same time as the apple crop.

    2 kilos (4lb 8 oz) medlars
    8 cloves
    4 lemons
    granulated sugar

1 Wash the fruit, halve and put in a jam pan, add the lemons quartered. Just cover with water and add the cloves. Bring to the boil and cook the fruit until mushy, strain through a jelly bag into a large bowl. At this stage the liquid looks milky and, frankly, slightly revolting.

2 Measure the liquid back into the jam pan and for every pint of juice, add a pound of sugar and a tablespoonful of lemon juice. Bring to the boil, stirring until the sugar has dissolved.

3 Begin to test the juice on a plate after 15 minutes and as soon as it shows signs of setting, turn off the heat. Skim the nasties from the surface and bottle in sterilized jars.

Serves 6 as a starter

Quality ham is essential; the flavours work when it's the delicious sort cut off the bone, and the meat is sweet and fresh. I am lucky enough to live near a butcher who must bake hams for Britain because he always seems to have a tray of cooked knuckles surrounded with flavoursome jelly and going for a song. This is the ideal meat with which to make potted ham or ham and pea soup.

approximately 300g (10½oz) ham

200g (7oz) unsalted butter

4 sage leaves and a few for decoration

fresh nutmeg

1 Pulverize the ham in a food processor. Melt the butter and add the 4 sage leaves, finely chopped; add some grated nutmeg.

2 Stir most of the butter mixture into the ham and pack into a suitable dish with a lid.

3 Pour the last remaining couple of tablespoonfuls of butter over the top and add a few sage leaves (this seals the ham from the air so that it can remain safely in the fridge for a few days).

Serve with peeled quails' eggs and fresh bread or toast rubbed with garlic and sprinkled with a little olive oil.

Pickled Pears

Makes 2 x 500ml (18 oz) kilner jars

Serve with cheese and cold meats. Ideal as part of a Boxing Day spread.

6 small firm Conference pears

500g (1lb 2 oz) granulated sugar

500ml (18 fl oz) cider vinegar

1 tsp allspice

1 tsp cloves

2 small cinnamon sticks

zest of a small orange

2 bay leaves

1 Pour the vinegar into a saucepan and stir in the sugar, bring to the boil and continue to stir until the sugar has dissolved. Add the allspice, cloves, cinnamon and orange zest and simmer for five minutes.

2 Peel and halve the pears. Add to the mixture and simmer for a further 10 minutes, turning occasionally. Lift the pears into sterilized jars. Boil the mixture for a further five minutes, adding the bay leaves at the last minute.

3 Pour over the pears, seal and store them for about eight weeks before use.

Venison Loin with Lardons and Prunes

Serves 4

Venison is plentiful in Gloucestershire. It's lean flavoursome meat, helped along by a fistful of lardons, alias fatty little cubes of bacon, preferably Old Spot.

700g venison loin or fillet

3tbsp olive oil

300ml (10 fl oz) red wine

2 garlic cloves, peeled and chopped

1 medium onion, peeled and chopped

115g (4 oz) fatty bacon cubes, Old Spot by choice

220g tin prunes in light syrup, stones out

3-4 sprigs fresh thyme

salt and pepper

Pre-heat oven to 180°C (350°F) gas mark 4

1 Stir 2 tablespoonfuls of olive oil, half the red wine and the two chopped garlic cloves together and add the thyme. Cut the venison into walnut-size cubes and marinate for at least two hours.

2 Heat the last tablespoonful of oil and gently soften the onion. Add the bacon pieces and finally the marinated meat, turning it so it's coloured on all sides. Put into a casserole with a lid.

3 Chop the prunes roughly and stir them with their juice into the casserole together with the rest of the red wine, the last of the marinade and a little salt and pepper.

4 Cover and cook for 45 minutes or until tender.

Serve with potato, carrot and swede mash with plenty of butter, chopped parsley and salt and pepper.

Pork Tenderloin stuffed with Thyme and Lemon

Serves 4

Pork tenderloin, like streaky bacon, must be one of the best-value cuts of meat on the market, although where streaky bacon is concerned I'm at a loss to know why we can't produce the Italian equivalent, a wafer thin pancetta that melts to a delectable nothingness in the pan.

1 pork tenderloin

75g (2¾oz) fresh breadcrumbs

small bunch fresh thyme

zest from a lemon

2 shallots, peeled and finely chopped

50g (1¾oz) butter

6 rashers pancetta or streaky bacon

sea salt and pepper

1 carrot, peeled and finely diced

150ml (7 floz) apple juice, medium

Pre-heat oven to 180°C (350°) gas mark 4

1 Trim any fat from the tenderloin and split it lengthways, but not all the way through, so that it opens like a book.

2 Mix the breadcrumbs, thyme leaves, and lemon zest. Soften half the butter in a pan and cook the shallots until soft but not brown. Mix with the rest of the stuffing and add a little salt and pepper. Pack the stuffing into the pork tenderloin and roll the strips of pancetta or bacon around the outside to keep it in place.

3 Put the pork on a shallow roasting tray, melt the remaining butter and pour it over the top. Sprinkle the diced carrot and a splash of the apple juice on the tray. Roast for an hour. Lift the pork on to a carving board and de-glaze the roasting pan with the remaining apple juice, adding a pinch of salt and some pepper. Serve with finely shredded buttery spring greens.

Pork and Perry Casserole

Serves 4

I have a husband who wears a guarded look when the word casserole is mentioned, but he succumbs readily to this particular marriage of pork, perry and thyme.

600g (1lb 5oz) pork shoulder

1 tbsp plain flour

1 tsp paprika

2 tbsp sunflower oil

2-3 shallots, peeled and chopped

¼ litre (9 fl oz) perry or apple juice

2 sprigs thyme

2 tbsp crème fraîche

sea salt and pepper

1 tbsp chopped parsley

Pre-heat oven to 180°C (350°) gas mark 4

1 Trim the pork into smallish cubes. Mix the flour with the paprika and dust the pork in the mixture.

2 Heat the oil in a frying pan and add the shallots, fry gently until softened. Add the pork and lightly brown on all sides, spoon the pork and shallots into a lidded casserole.

3 Pour the perry into the frying pan and incorporate all the meat juices, add to the casserole together with the sprigs of thyme. Cover the casserole and cook for 60 minutes or until the pork is tender.

4 Remove from the oven, stir in the crème fraîche, salt and pepper to taste and return to the oven for a further 10-15 minutes. Sprinkle with some chopped parsley.

Serve with jacket potatoes.

Chicken Breasts in Sweet Peppers, White Wine and Rosemary

Serves 4-6

This is a perennial favourite of mine; each flavour tells its own story. A dry white wine, born and bred in Gloucestershire works perfectly, but don't use anything oaky in flavour. I like to use a wok.

2 yellow peppers

2 red sweet peppers

4 free-range chicken breasts

50g (1¾ oz) butter

2 tbs olive oil

2 garlic cloves

300ml (½ pt) white wine

2 sprigs rosemary

salt and black pepper

450g (1lb) fresh tagliatelli

Pre-heat oven to 190°C (375°F) gas mark 5

1 Wrap the peppers in foil and cook in the top of the oven for 25-30 minutes. When cool, pull out the pepper stalks, split the peppers and scrape away the seeds, dry on kitchen paper.

2 Skin the chicken breasts and cut into chunky strips.

3 Heat the butter and 1 tablespoonful of oil in a heavy pan, fry the meat lightly on both sides. Peel, crush and add the garlic followed by the wine. Cover the pan and cook slowly for 15 minutes.

4 Slice the peppers and add to the pan with the rosemary. Add the seasoning and continue cooking slowly for a further 20 minutes. Meanwhile put a large serving dish in the oven to warm and prepare a big pan of lightly salted boiling water, adding the remaining tbsp of olive oil.

5 Cook the tagliatelli for 6-7 minutes until al dente, strain, toss into the pan of meat and peppers and serve immediately.

Chilli Lamb Kebabs with Yoghurt, Mint and Garlic Sauce

Serves 4

Quick to prepare, delicious, and can be cooked indoors or on a barbecue. The yoghurt and mint sauce is a sprightly foil to the lamb and chilli.

Kebabs

500g (1lb 2oz) minced lamb

2 green chillies, de-seeded and finely chopped

½ tsp cinnamon

juice of ½ lemon

2 tbsp fresh white breadcrumbs

a medium onion or an echalion shallot, peeled and diced

2 tbsp sunflower oil

sea salt and pepper

Yoghurt, mint and garlic sauce

150g (5½oz) yoghurt

1 tbsp fresh mint, finely chopped

juice of ½ lemon

1 peeled and crushed garlic clove

1 tbsp extra virgin olive oil

sea salt and pepper

1 Put the lamb into a large mixing bowl and add the chillies, cinnamon, lemon juice and breadcrumbs. Heat 1 tablespoonful of oil and gently fry the onion or shallot until soft. Spoon into the lamb mixture and add a couple of good pinches of sea salt and some ground pepper. Mix together thoroughly.

2 Roll the meat into balls or sausage shapes and thread on to skewers. Heat the remaining tablespoonful of oil in a large frying pan and cook the kebabs, turning occasionally until they are golden all the way round.

3 To make the sauce, mix together all the ingredients and serve with the kebabs.

Beef Carpaccio

Serves 4

The most delicate of summer dishes as either a starter, main course or light lunch. You can either use a top quality, trimmed sirloin steak – or as a little goes a long way, buy a chunk of middle-cut beef fillet when not a scrap is wasted and the result is guaranteed melt-in-the-mouth.

450g (1lb) beef fillet

olive oil

balsamic vinegar

shavings of fresh parmesan cheese

salad leaves

salt and pepper

1 Wrap the fillet and put it in the freezer for about an hour until the meat is firm enough to cut into thin slices. Cut a few large sheets of baking parchment and place four or five slices of beef on each sheet and then cover it with another sheet.

2 Using a meat mallet or something similar, tap the meat out until wafer thin. Peel off the paper, spread the meat on the serving plates, decorate with a few shavings of parmesan and small salad leaves including rocket.

3 Trickle over a little good olive oil and tiny splashes of balsamic vinegar or soy sauce; season with a grind of sea salt and black pepper.

Serves 2 as a starter

The Scandinavians have the upper hand when it comes to serving smoked eel; there is little better way of eating it that to lay it on a slice of rye bread with a frippery of salad, horseradish and a little grated beetroot pickle.

It's easy to make: dissolve a tablespoonful of caster sugar with a drop of boiling water and add a tablespoon of red wine vinegar and a little salt. Grate a cooked beetroot and steep in the vinegar for about an hour. Drain and serve.

100g smoked eel

2 slices rye bread

salad leaves

hard boiled egg – optional

horseradish

pickled beetroot

Wash it down with a shot of iced aquavit or vodka, or a glass of cider or perry.

Trout Fillets Spiced with Soy, Honey and Mustard

Serves 4

A simple, spicy way of cooking trout or salmon fillets, and they can be eaten hot or cold. The marinade is also excellent for chicken fillets, particularly for barbecuing or cooking in a cast-iron ribbed grill pan.

2 trout, weighing a pound or more each, filleted

marinade

> 2 tbsp soy sauce
> 2 tbsp sunflower oil
> 2 tsp runny honey
> ½ tsp grainy mustard
> ½ tsp chilli powder
> ½ lime, squeezed

for cooking

> 1 tbsp sunflower oil
> 150ml (5 fl oz) apple juice to de-glaze the pan

1 Whisk the marinade ingredients together, dip the trout fillets and then lay them face down in a dish. Pour over the remainder of the marinade and refrigerate for a couple of hours.

2 Heat the sunflower oil in a large frying pan. Add the trout fillets, again face down and cook for 2-3 minutes each side. Whilst the fillets are cooking add a few spoonfuls of the marinade and gradually pour in the apple juice. The marinade caramelises quickly so keep slowly adding the apple to help to keep the juices liquid. Pour any remaining cooking juices over the fish and serve immediately.

Trout is always good with sliced steamed fennel with butter, sea salt and grated nutmeg.

Plum Purée with Ginger Crème Fraîche and Cinnamon Meringues

Serves 6

This is a sybarite's pudding. The purée can be plum or rhubarb as the season dictates – and the meringues made in advance and kept in an airtight tin.

Fruit purée

450g (1lb) plums

100g granulated or caster sugar

3 tbsp crème fraîche

3 knobs crystalized ginger and a little syrup

De-stone and stew the plums with just enough water to cover the bottom of the pan together with the sugar, stirring until the sugar has dissolved. Cook for a further couple of minutes. Purée the fruit.

Chop the ginger into small pieces and mix with the crème fraîche and a little of the ginger syrup. Spoon some of this mixture into the bottom of each glass or dish. Add the purée and top with three or four meringues.

Cinnamon meringues

2 egg whites, room temperature

100g (3½ oz) caster sugar

1 tsp lemon juice

¼ tsp ground cinnamon

Pre-heat oven to 140ºC (284ºF) gas mark 1

Using a large clean bowl, whisk the egg whites, gradually adding the sugar, a dash of lemon juice and finally the cinnamon. The whites should stand up in peaks. To make little meringues to sit on top of a fruit purée, put teaspoonfuls onto a baking sheet and set on the top shelf of the oven for two hours. Store in an airtight tin when cold.

Oldbury Tarts

Makes 24

Mrs Sue Taylor is from a Gloucestershire family. Her grandmother made Oldbury Tarts on a Saturday night, ready for Sunday, but it was Sue's great aunt Edie who showed Sue the secrets involved in making these delicious tarts. There are three basic tips. The gooseberries must be the hard green variety, not too ripe. Using a hot water crust pastry, make the tarts and let them stand overnight before cooking the following day. Don't be in a hurry!

  450g (1lb) plain flour
  100g (3½oz) lard
  100g (3½oz) butter
  200ml (7floz) boiling water
  450g (1lb) small firm gooseberries, topped and tailed
  caster sugar
  muscovado sugar

1 Sieve the flour into a bowl and cut the fat into small pieces, add to the flour. Pour over the boiling water and knife the mixture together until the dough is pliable.

2 To make each pie, take one knob of pastry the size of a walnut to form the main shell, and another the size of a hazelnut to form the top. Roll each piece very thinly on a floured board. Shape the larger piece to form a cup for the fruit, stand it upright and crimp the edges. Drop 4-5 gooseberries into each case and add a small teaspoonful of white sugar and a small teaspoonful of Muscovado sugar to each. Put the top on and pinch around the edges to seal. Make two knife slits in the top of each pie and stand overnight.

3 Pre-heat the oven to 200°C (400°F) gas mark 6.

4 Make a sugar-syrup with 1tsp brown sugar and ½ cup boiling water. Put the pies into the top of the oven for 15 minutes; spoon a drop of the syrup into each pie and return the pies to the oven for a further fifteen minutes or until the pastry is golden. Serve cold.

Apple Tart

Serves 6-8

A friend gave me this classic apple tart recipe; it's the sort that always looks so enticing in the windows of patisseries, thin and elegant with a dusting of icing sugar.

> 6 Coxes apples
> 375g (13 oz) flaky pastry
> 1 tbsp plain flour
> 50g (1¾ oz) melted butter
> 100g (3½ oz) caster sugar
> 2 tsp lemon juice
> cinnamon
> icing sugar to serve

Pre-heat oven to 220°C (425°F) gas mark 7

1 Line a 26cm (10") flan tin with a removable base with baking parchment and butter the sides of the tin.

2 Roll out the pastry and line the tin. Sprinkle the base of the pastry with the flour – this stops the pastry becoming soggy during cooking. Peel, core and finely slice the apples into a bowl, spooning on most of the sugar as you go. Pour over the lemon juice, add the melted butter and turn the fruit.

3 Arrange the apple slices round and round the tart. Sprinkle with cinnamon and the remaining sugar. Bake for about an hour, until the pastry is crisp and the fruit just beginning to caramelise on the edges.

Serve warm with cream.

Apple Day Cake

Makes 16-20 portions

This cake has evolved around spring visits to an orchard blossom party at which the hosts build the bonfire of old apple wood, cook sausages and serve cider, made from the previous year's crop. The cake is big and good-tempered and lasts for days. I use one of the new silicone moulds with crinkly edges but a tin will do just as well.

300g (10 oz) plain flour

175g (6 oz) wholemeal flour

225g (8 oz) light brown muscovado sugar

1 tsp cinnamon

1 orange – juice and finely grated zest

2 tsp baking powder

½ tsp baking soda

1 tsp salt

175ml (6 fl oz) sunflower oil

3 eggs

150ml (¼ pt) milk

3 Coxes or Golden Delicious apples, peeled, cored and finely chopped

75g (2½ oz) walnuts, chopped

Pre-heat oven to 170°C (325°F) gas mark 3

1 Measure the flours, sugar, cinnamon, orange zest, baking powder, baking soda and salt and sift into a large mixing bowl. Pour in the sunflower oil and mix with your fingers until the cake is crumby. Whisk the eggs and milk together and stir into the bowl. Fold in the chopped apples and walnuts. Spoon into a buttered mould, put the mould on a baking tray and cook for 75-80 minutes on the top shelf; pierce with a skewer and if it comes out clean, the cake is done.

2 Leave in the tin or mould for 10 minutes, turn on to a cake rack until just warm, then transfer to a plate before glazing.

Glaze

100g (3½oz) light brown muscovado sugar

juice of a fresh orange

75g (2¼oz) butter

icing sugar for decoration

Mix the first three ingredients in a small saucepan and bring to the boil, simmer gently for a minute and spoon slowly over the cake. Dust with icing sugar just before serving.

Walnut Bread

For a large plaited loaf

You can't beat a fine selection of Gloucestershire cheese, homemade walnut bread with a bowl of salad and a bottle of perry or cider.

450g (1lb) strong white flour

1 level tsp doves farm quick yeast (or similar)

2 tsp sea salt, rubbed in the palms of your hands to break down the crystals

100g (3½ oz) walnut pieces

175ml (6 fl oz) boiling water

1 tsp malt extract (health food shops)

150ml (5 fl oz) cold water

1 tbsp walnut oil

1 Mix the flour, yeast, walnut pieces and salt together in a large bowl.

2 Pour the boiling water into a measuring jug, stir in the malt extract. Add the cold water and walnut oil.

3 Make a well in the centre of the flour and using dough hooks, slowly mix in the liquid with the flour until all the liquid is used up and the flour is incorporated. Kneed the dough a little more by hand, adding flour if it seems too sticky. Once the dough is pliable, put into a large clean bowl and cover with cling film or a cloth. Leave in a warm place, usually for about a couple of hours or until the dough has doubled in size.

4 With floury hands, kneed the dough once more and put into an oiled bread tin or on a heavy baking tray. To plait the loaf on the tray, shape the dough into an oblong, cut it into three strips leaving just the top bit uncut. Plait and tuck the newly-plaited end bits under the loaf. Cover the loaf again until it rises and decorate with a few walnut halves.

5 Pre-heat the oven to 220ºC (425ºF) gas mark 7.

6 Half fill a baking tray with water and put it in the bottom of the oven to create steam during baking. Bake
   the bread for 35-40 minutes until the bottom sounds hollow when tapped.

Elderflower Cordial

Makes about a litre

Plan in advance! Citric acid always seems to be in short supply when the elderflowers are out. This year's excuse was that dealers were cutting it into their cocaine, but surely nothing like that would happen in Gloucestershire? Although the fridge life of this cordial in only about a month, it freezes well and can then be used at any time of year.

15-20 elderflower blossoms

2 lemons

1½ kilos (3lb 5oz) granulated sugar

1.2 litres (2 pints) water

50g (1¾oz) citric or tartaric acid

1 Slice the lemons. Boil the sugar and water, stirring until the sugar has dissolved, stir in the citric acid and let the liquid cool.

2 Give the elderflowers a shake to remove bugs and put into a large mixing bowl with the lemon slices. Pour over the sugar syrup, cover and steep for 24 hours in a cool place. Strain through muslin into a jug and fill sterilized bottles.

Madeleines

Makes about 20

Light, buttery little shell-shaped cakes, often flavoured with orange, lemon or vanilla and the subject of a dialogue by Marcel Proust in *Remembrance of Things Past*. The particular episode occured when he is having tea with his mother. 'I declined at first, and then for no particular reason, changed my mind. She sent for one of those squat, plump little cakes called 'petites madeleines', which look as though they've been moulded in the fluted valve of a scallop shell'. Proust then takes a morsel of cake that he's soaked in his tea and relishes its dazzling effects – which he likens to those of being in love. I can't guarantee these will produce similar results, but they are delicious with fruit fools or dunked into fruit liqueurs or dessert wines. *To make them you'll need a special tin, called a dariole mould, available in kitchen shops.*

    3 large eggs
    125g (4½oz) caster sugar
    finely grated zest of an orange
    125g (4½oz) butter, melted but not hot
    100g (3½oz) self raising flour
    1 tbsp ground almond

Pre-heat oven to 190°C (375°F) gas mark 5.

1 Beat the eggs, sugar and orange zest together until the mixture is almost as thick as a mousse. Slowly whisk in the melted butter and fold in the flour and ground almond.

2 Butter the moulds and spoon in the mixture.

3 Bake for 15 minutes or until golden, and cool on a cake rack. Sprinkle with icing sugar before serving.

They are best eaten the same day or frozen then thawed a couple of hours before eating. I serve them with rhubarb and ginger fool.

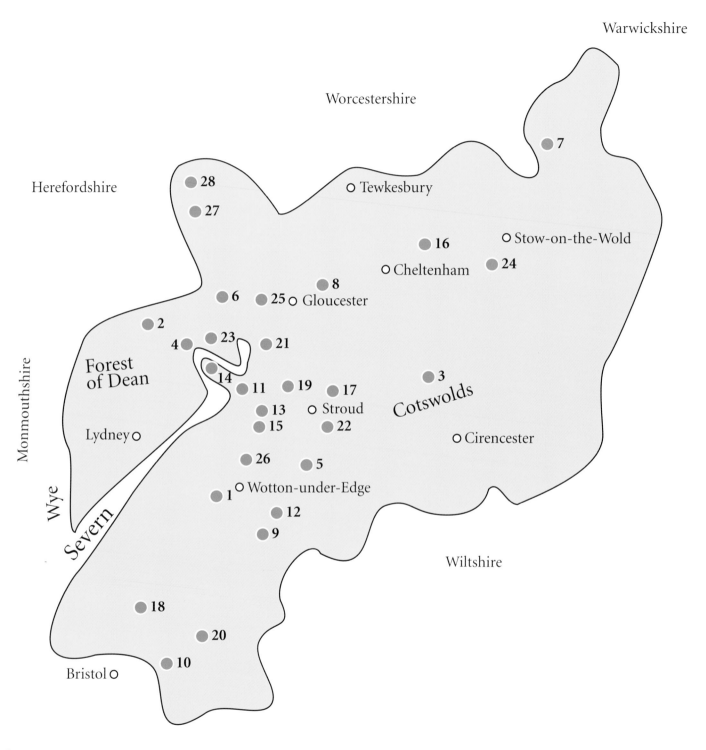

Warwickshire

Worcestershire

Herefordshire

● **28**

● **27**

○ Tewkesbury

● **7**

● **16**

○ Stow-on-the-Wold

○ Cheltenham

● **24**

● **8**

● **6**   ● **25** ○ Gloucester

● **2**

Monmouthshire

● **4**   ● **23**

● **21**

Forest
of Dean

● **3**

● **14**

Cotswolds

Wye

● **11**   ● **19**   ● **17**

● **13**   ○ Stroud

Lydney ○

● **15**   ● **22**

○ Cirencester

Severn

● **26**   ● **5**

● **1** ○ Wotton-under-Edge

● **12**

Wiltshire

● **9**

● **18**

● **20**

● **10**

Bristol ○

Where to find the producers

number on map followed by *page number*

SHOPS

Beef

British Blue Beef
Richard and Julia Carter
Tyning Ash
Uley Lane
Coaley
GL11 5AW
Tel: 01453 860072
'Leaner-than-normal', tender beef.
Animals home-bred, home-fed, all cereals
grown on their farm.

Cheese

Hania Cheeses (Cheese Suppliers)
Middle Crescent
Middle Hill
Stroud
GL6 8BE
Tel: 01453 884320

House of Cheese
Church Street
Tetbury
GL8 8JG
Tel: 01666 502865
www.houseofcheese.co.uk
Cheese and all that accompanies it.
Wedding cheeses a speciality.

Delicatessens

Hunter and Todd
Delicatessen and Wine
High Street
Newnham-on-Severn
GL14 1BB
Tel: 01594 516211

www.hunterandtodd.co.uk
Monday-Saturday 8.00am-7.00pm
Cheeses, meats, chutneys

Maby's Food and Wine
Digbeth Street
Stow-on-the-Wold
Cheltenham
Gloucestershire GL54 1BN
Tel: 01451 870071
Local produce.
Homemade ready meals.
Open: Monday-Thursday 9.30am-5.30pm
Friday and Saturday 9.00am-5.30pm

Sunshine Health Foods
25 Church Street
Stroud
Gloucestershire GL5 1JL
Tel: 01453 763923
Jim Dickenson's honey.

William's Fish Market and Foodhall
3 Fountain Street
Nailsworth
Gloucestershire GL6 0BL
Tel: 01453 832240
www.williamsfoodhall.co.uk
Produce includes ham and bacon and ham
locally cured and smoked in nearby
Woodchester.
Local cheeses include Charles Martell's
Stinking Bishop and Jonathan Crump's
Single and Double Gloucester.
Delicious brunches and lunches.
Open: 9.00am-5.00pm Monday-Saturday

Eggs

Sherston Free Range Eggs
Bruce and Gail Hamilton
Home Farm
Knockdown
Tetbury
GL8 8QT
Tel: 01454 23803, 07973 634457
Email: home.farm@ukgateway.net

Farm Shops

David Anthony and Sandie Ham
25 Westerleigh Road
Heathfield
Bristol
BS16 9RB
Game in season, pork, lamb, home-cured
ham, local vegetables

Puddleditch Farm Shop
Berkeley Heath
Berkeley
GL12 9EU
Tel: 01453 810816
Hen and duck eggs
Homemade chutneys, quiches, jams.
Berkeley estate venison and local meats.

Stancombe Beech Farm Shop
Stancombe Lane
Stroud
GL6 7NF
Tel: 01452 771077
Potatoes, seasonal farm vegetables, Jim
Dickenson's honey.
Open: Monday-Wednesday 8.30am-1.00pm